The Simple Guide to Buying a Dental Practice
& Getting a Great Deal

The Simple Guide to Buying a Dental Practice & Getting a Great Deal

By Manfred Purtzki, CPA, CA

Blue Beetle Books

First published, 2022
Trade paperback ISBN: 978-1-7778287-2-1

Blue Beetle Books Inc., Victoria, B.C.
www.bluebeetlebooks.com
Tel: 250.704.6686

Inquiries regarding requests to reprint all or part of *The Simple Guide to Buying a Dental Practice and Getting a Great Deal* should be addressed to Manfred Purtzki at:

Purtzki Transitions Inc.
1700-570 Granville Street
Vancouver, BC
V6C 3P1
Tel: 778-288-2920
Email: manfred@purtzki.com

It is recommended that legal, accounting, and other professional advice is sought before acting on any information contained in this book as each individual's financial circumstances are unique.

Written in collaboration with Mike Wicks.
Cover design and book layout by Tom Spetter.
Editor: Kara Anderson
Custom publishing services provided by Blue Beetle Books Inc.

Contents

Introduction XI

Chapter 1: Planning the Practice Purchase 3

  The Self-Assessment 4

  The Challenges Ahead 5

    The Money Challenge 5

    The Self-Confidence Challenge 5

    The Fear of Failure Challenge 6

    The Spouse Challenge 6

    The Associateship Challenge 6

  Buying a Dental Practice—Winning Strategies 6

    Strategy #1: Get Into the Right Headspace 6

    Strategy #2: Get Into the Seller's Headspace 7

    Strategy #3: Understand the True Value of the Practice 8

    Strategy #4: Develop a Good Negotiating Strategy 8

    Strategy #5: Budget Carefully 9

    Strategy #6: Have an Antidote to Rose-Tinted Glasses 9

  Assembling Your Transition Team 10

    The Accountant 11

The Lawyer. 11

The Dental Practice Acquisition Expert. 11

Key Takeaways. 12

Chapter 2: Exploring Purchasing Opportunities 15

Watching the Listings. 15

The Entrepreneurial Alternative 17

The Proactive Approach. 18

Step One – Where do You Want to Work?. 18

Step Two – Create a Database 18

Step Three – Identify Likely Candidates 19

Step Four – Send an Introductory Letter. 19

Step Five – First Meeting Preparation 20

Step Six – The Practice Visit. 22

Key Takeaways. 25

Chapter 3: Investigating the Purchase Opportunity 27

Types of Sale. 27

Straight Sale 27

Seller/Associate Sale 28

Partnership Interest Sale. 28

Putting the Practice on the Hoist 29

The Practice Valuation 29

Finding the Diamond in the Rough 31

The Break-Even Analysis: An Indispensable Tool in
Finding an Excellent Practice 32

Location 34

Demographics 34

Patient Information. 35

Type of Work 35

Facility Lease 35

Team Profile. 35

Management Information System 36

SWOT Analysis 36

Key Takeaways. 37

Chapter 4: The Letter of Intent (LOI) 39

Case Study: Melissa. 39

Case Study: Steven 40

The Real Estate Question 41

Overview 42

Composition of the Letter of Intent 42

The Purchase Price 42

The Deposit 43

The List of Assets. 43

Accounts Receivable 44

The Closing Date. 44

Non-Competition/Non-Solicitation. 44

Associateship 44

Conditions Precedent 45

Patient Retreatment Clause 45

Employees. 45

Transition 45

Due Diligence 46

Key Takeaways 46

Chapter 5: Due Diligence 47

Case Study: Jordan 47

Due Diligence Audit 50

Key Takeaways 54

Chapter 6: Before You Sign the Purchase Agreement 55

Practice Revenues 56

Premises Lease 56

Financing the Purchase 57

Knowing the Workplace Culture 58

The Purchase Agreement Dissected 60

Key Takeaways 64

Chapter 7: Purchasing a Partial Interest 67

Solo Group Practice 67

The Cost-Sharing Arrangement 69

The Buy-Sell Agreement 71

Partnership 74

Key Takeaways 75

Chapter 8: Your First 30 Days of Practice Ownership 77

Controlling Your Overhead 78

The Office Manager: A Lynchpin 79

Creating a Championship Team 80

Hiring Staff. 81

Managing Staff. 81

Out of the Box Thinking 82

Key Takeaways. 83

Chapter 9: The Road to Financial Success 85

Focusing on Growth—First Steps. 85

Financial Habits For Highly Successful Practice Owners 87

Live Within Your Means. 87

Set Firm Goals 87

Execute Your Plan 88

Monitor Progress. 88

Pay Yourself First 89

Invest Aggressively But Wisely 89

Practice Sensible Buying. 90

Reward Yourself!. 90

Key Takeaways. 90

Acknowledgements 93

I

Introduction

After publishing my first book, *The Simple Guide to Selling Your Dental Practice for More Money*, I realized how many dentists are looking for guidance on buying a practice. In many ways, buying a dental practice can be more challenging than selling one. The biggest challenge for many is finding a suitable practice opportunity. In a competitive market, good dental clinics are often snatched up the day they are listed, and multiple offers at or above listing price are common.

If you have been searching for a good clinic for a long time, you may be tempted to throw caution to the wind and only conduct a superficial examination of the pros and cons when you find one that looks like a good fit. Never fall in love with a clinic. Treat it like buying a car; put it up on the hoist and conduct a thorough inspection. You must carry out a risk assessment using tools like a SWOT (Strengths, Weaknesses, Opportunities, and Threats) analysis. Then, if you spot anything of significant concern, walk away!

If you are reading this, you are probably an associate. Being an associate is a good thing as it allows you time to hone your technical skills and learn about practice management. Learn as much as you can about the business of dentistry. Take business courses to learn about practice management and reading financial statements. I'm not suggesting that you take an MBA, but knowing your practice's management accounts and learning when you need to take appropriate remedial action is critical to your financial success. Don't rush through your associateship phase unless you're convinced that you're ready to become a practice owner.

Whatever your situation, before you start looking at listings, take a step back and question whether moving from the relative safety of working as an associate to owning your own clinic is something you are fully prepared to embrace. I can hear you saying, "Of course, it's my dream; it's the obvious next career step. I want the autonomy, the prestige, and of course the financial rewards." All of which is sound thinking. Owning your own practice is without question the right move—unless that is, you ignore the reality that once you take over the reins of a clinic, you cease to be an associate. The days of turning up for work, seeing patients all day, practising the art of dentistry, and keeping your head down, are irrevocably over the minute a seller hands you the keys to your new practice.

I have seen so many new owners forget that their primary role is to manage their clinic. Sure, they still have to see patients, but now they also have to keep the ship afloat. Not everyone is suited to dealing with building practice revenues, hiring and firing staff, money management and fiscal responsibility, maintenance issues, and the inevitable office politics, all while leading a team of dedicated employees. Are you?

Sorry to scare you or be a downer, but the best thing I can do to help you is to give you a reality check before you borrow a ton of money and commit to a life-changing, albeit potentially life-enhancing, decision. Don't be too worried, in *The Simple Guide to Buying a Dental Practice and Getting a Great Deal*, I'll help you navigate some of the dangerous waters ahead of you.

If you are still reading you now know what you're getting into, so here's the good news: you can earn twice as much being an owner than you can as an associate, as long as you don't make too many mistakes along the way.

As I mentioned, dental practice inventory is tight in some regions, so you may be forced to lighten up on your criteria and consider less than ideal locations. For instance, there is more competition for urban clinics than less expensive rural clinics. Alternatively, you may need to consider a partnership deal. Partnership deals are becoming increasingly popular, especially with dentists concerned about work-life balance. It's a minefield out there, but there are many ways to minimize risk and never lose sight of the fact that the rewards can be significant.

You can employ several stratagems to help you navigate safely through this challenging terrain. First, pull together a professional team that understands dental transitions; second, carry out sufficient due diligence; and third, never let your heart rule your head. Always be prepared to walk away from a deal that doesn't seem right.

When I started writing this book, I thought I would stick solely to guiding you toward all the things you need to know to buy the best possible practice at the right price and do it safely. After seven chapters I felt I'd completed that task, but then realized that I'd left you alone with the keys in your hand standing outside your new clinic. I think you deserve more.

I would hate to have helped you buy an outstanding practice, only to see you get into serious trouble over the subsequent weeks or months. For this reason, I added chapter eight, which is a checklist of critical things you need to do during your first thirty days of ownership. During my twenty-plus years as a dental transitions specialist, I've seen dentists succeed beyond their wildest dreams, and I've seen them turn a once-thriving clinic into a shambles. Work *on* your dental practice, as well as *in* it, and before long you'll be driving your Maserati GranTurismo along the Amalfi Coast of Italy while your office manager supervises the four associates you have working in your practice.

In the final chapter, I don my CPA hat to show you how to build a better life for yourself and your family by taking control of your business and your money, and how you can retire earlier and wealthier than you could have ever imagined, all while doing the job you love.

And it all starts with a key ring holding a golden tooth.

The Simple Guide to Buying a Dental Practice & Getting a Great Deal

Planning the Practice Purchase

Have you thought about purchasing your own dental practice? Perhaps you graduated a year or two ago and have been working as an associate so you can pay down your student loans. You are committed to your profession and are determined to succeed—to make a difference. Working as an associate is a great way to begin your career, but it can also be limiting. You are probably handling patients with less complex care needs that are less interesting and less financially beneficial. If you are ambitious, you will want to stretch yourself professionally and as a businessperson. Buying a dental practice may be exciting and help you do that, but it can also be risky. You are not alone; most graduating dentists and associates dream of owning a dental practice one day and building it into a success beyond their expectations.

Purchasing a dental practice is a significant commitment, one you should not take lightly. The golden key is to find a clinic that is right for you—and to do it the first time. There are no do-overs; with the right practice you can make lots of money and have fun along the way, but choose unwisely and it can be a career-buster. The grief and the financial consequences of getting into a bad deal can be devastating.

Now you are suitably scared and thinking, "being an associate may not be so bad after all," let me assure you that I can lead you safely through the minefield of buying a practice and help you get the best deal possible. It's what I do.

The Self-Assessment

First, you need to take a step back—way back—and make sure owning a practice is something you really want to do. That practice you've seen advertised is like the golden retriever pup at the shelter with big brown eyes begging you to take it home. They have a lot in common; they are long-term commitments requiring constant attention. On the other hand, they can also be incredibly rewarding. You just need to know the scope of what you are taking on—the good, the bad, and the poopy. Does owning a dental practice suit your personal goals, aspirations, and capabilities?

Answering the questions below will give you insight into whether this career path is right for you. Be honest with yourself and write your answers down— there is space at the end of the book. Be truthful—no one is looking.

- ☐ Why do I want to purchase a practice? Am I looking to earn more money, be my own boss, or am I looking to challenge myself professionally? Or perhaps, if you are honest with yourself, it's because you can't stand the dentist you are working for, or you are envious of fellow graduates who have opened their own practices.

- ☐ Do I possess an entrepreneurial drive? Am I excited by the idea of running a business? Am I willing to accept the risk of ownership and take full responsibility for the success or failure of my practice? Do I have the business acumen necessary? If not, am I willing to educate myself in what it takes to run a business?

- ☐ What type of dentistry do I enjoy? What are my long-term professional goals? Will owning a practice help me achieve these goals? Are there other options that will meet my needs?

- ☐ Where do I want to commit to living for the foreseeable future? Where would my spouse and children choose to live?

- ☐ Am I willing to make the necessary sacrifices in terms of the time and energy required to build up the practice?

- ☐ Do I have the confidence in my leadership abilities and practice management skills to be a successful business owner? Am I prepared to learn the business skills of becoming a team leader, communicating with patients, and assuming the role of CEO of my practice?

☐ Do I want, or need, to practice with an experienced dentist for their mentorship and sharing of management responsibilities? Do I want to consider joining a group?

☐ Am I ready and willing to make a significant financial commitment? Am I prepared to spend the next fifteen years on the treadmill, paying off a house mortgage and practice loans? How will that impact the lifestyle I want to lead?

☐ Will I be able to mentally cope with the financial exposure that buying a dental practice necessitates?

☐ What are my spouse's career needs? Have I considered them?

☐ What are my children's education needs?

☐ Can I count on the unwavering support of my spouse, particularly during the start-up phase of practice ownership?

Look back at your answers. Have you been honest with yourself?

The Challenges Ahead

No one said this was going to be easy. There are a bunch of hurdles that you will need to overcome if you choose to embark on this journey, so let's get them out of the way. Don't worry, none of them are insurmountable.

The Money Challenge

If you are an associate with ballooning student loans and a house mortgage, the idea of borrowing a million dollars to purchase a practice can be daunting. However, the extra income you can earn as an owner will be enough to pay back the purchase loan within a 7 to 10-year time frame. Practice ownership is an excellent investment.

The Self-Confidence Challenge

You may feel that you are not an entrepreneur, and that managing a practice is outside your comfort zone. The truth is you don't need to be an Elon Musk or an Arianna Huffington to run a dental practice. What you need is a dose of common sense, a willingness to work hard, and the desire to put the needs of your patients and staff ahead of your own. If you surround yourself with a team of capable advisors, you will be on your way to making ownership a reality.

The Fear of Failure Challenge

There is a degree of risk in everything we do; no matter how thoroughly you investigate the practice you are considering purchasing, you can never guarantee that it's a sure winner. However, many dentists overestimate the risks when buying a practice. One common misconception is the number of patients they will lose during a transition to the new ownership—it's lower than you might think.

The Spouse Challenge

A word of warning: if your spouse doesn't like the location of the practice you are considering purchasing, don't buy it—you need to decide jointly. Having your spouse on your side will save you a lot of grief, not to mention the possibility of a costly future practice relocation.

The Associateship Challenge

It is common for new dentists, suffocating under a $300,000 student loan, to continue working as an associate until their student debt has been repaid. On the face of it, this sounds like a sensible plan, but if you want to pay off your loan quickly, consider becoming an owner as soon as you can. Use a short-term associateship to hone your clinical and patient communication skills, but enjoy the benefits of ownership as soon as is feasible.

The financial benefit of taking the early practice ownership route is significant. By staying an associate rather than becoming an owner, your lost opportunity cost is about $10,000 per month.

Buying a Dental Practice—Winning Strategies

Now that you know some of the challenges you'll face when buying a dental practice, let me share some strategies to help you achieve your ambitions.

Strategy #1: Get Into the Right Headspace

Finding a practice requires dedication and a serious time commitment. It can take a year or two to find a suitable dental practice. Take it from me, you will experience a rollercoaster of emotions along the way, and will consider quitting and remaining in your associateship many times before you eventually find your new career home.

It will not be easy; you will need to juggle your job and your search for a clinic. It will be stressful. You will need to devote time to researching opportunities. If you limit your search to checking the listings, you could wait a long time before finding a practice that meets your needs. Many good dental practices are sold privately and are never widely advertised, so getting outside assistance may be a good idea. Not everyone has this level of commitment—it will test you. If you fail, it might indicate that running your own business is not for you, or at least not at this juncture.

It is essential to do some soul-searching before deciding to go out on your own. Sit down and seriously consider whether this is something you want to do—make no mistake, this is a life-changing decision. You will be running a business, not just practising dentistry. Consider what it will feel like to owe the bank hundreds of thousands of dollars. Talk to your significant other, how do they feel about joining you on this journey?

Getting into the right headspace also means thinking through what type of dental practice will fit your personality, work style, and the kind of dentistry you want to practice. Draft a description of your perfect practice. List all the non-negotiable things, and then create a second list of nice-to-haves so that you and your broker, if you hire one, know what you're looking for in the business. Then be patient and don't fall into the FOMO trap (Fear Of Missing Out). After a long search process, I have seen dentists overcome with fear of missing out on practice ownership. When that happens, those non-negotiable items lose their importance, and warning signs are ignored when evaluating practices. Remember, it's better to walk away than end up paying a ton of money and rueing the day you bought the practice.

Strategy #2: Get Into the Seller's Headspace

Once you start meeting sellers, it is a good idea to make an effort to understand their motivations and how emotionally attached they are to their practice. What concerns do they have about the practice's future under new ownership?

The key to dealing with sellers is to be modest and respectful of what they may have spent their whole career building. During your first meeting with them commit to deep listening; only speak when asking questions or gaining clarification. Your goal should be to understand their motivation for selling, learn how the practice operates, recognize any apprehension about selling, and identify any red flags. In sales, they say, sell yourself first. It is the same when buying a practice. You need to gain the confidence of the seller so that they would feel happy entrusting you with their staff and patients.

Strategy #3: Understand the True Value of the Practice

Be conservative when forecasting the practice's future cash flow. Ensure you run financial forecasts and focus on bottom-line cash flow. Carry out a thorough estimate of future capital expenses, including high tech investments, upgrading dental equipment and leaseholds, and your upcoming working capital requirements.

Lastly, don't be overly enthusiastic—it is unlikely there will be a magical increase in revenues as soon as you take over. Be cautious with your revenue projections.

Once you understand the true value proposition you can judge how much the practice is worth. It is better to overpay for a good practice than get a poor one for cheap.

Strategy #4: Develop a Good Negotiating Strategy

Negotiation is not a zero-sum game, and if you try to make it so you will likely end up on the losing side. While a win-win situation might seem good, buying a practice is business, and you need to ensure you get a great deal while remaining ethical and above board. There is a balance; if you manage to pull one over on the seller there might be damaging ramifications. When you purchase a practice you will need the outgoing dentist and their staff to introduce you to patients, or potentially continue to work with you as an associate. The relationship you build while negotiating the sale is of vital importance.

If possible, use a third party to negotiate the sale, such as a transition specialist and a lawyer to handle the technical aspects of the negotiations. These experts are beneficial if there is any contentious issue.

A good negotiation strategy starts with creating a list of need-to-haves, a wish list, and any deal-breakers. At the same time, put yourself in the seller's shoes and consider what their list might contain.

Finally, look at what benefits you might offer the seller, such as an associate position after the sale or a family member's employment.

Negotiation only gets you so far. Once you have an agreement, everything needs to be recorded in the contract by your lawyer. Well-written, comprehensive, win-win contracts form the foundation of great deals and ongoing relationships.

Strategy #5: Budget Carefully

I suggested earlier that buying a practice sooner rather than later made financial sense. Now I am going to balance that with a warning: I have seen many first-time practice buyers blow all their available cash on the purchase price, leaving them short when it comes to other unexpected expenses.

Work out a budget for your practice purchase. It should take into consideration not only the cost of buying the practice, but also include things like the cost of replacing employees who leave, training those replacements, patient attrition, the temporary reduction in the number of patients you can see while assuming the role of CEO of your business, and anything that might come out of left field. A budget will give you a good idea of your capital needs and what line of credit you will need from the bank.

Strategy #6: Have an Antidote to Rose-Tinted Glasses

It's easy to get carried away when launching out on your own for the first time. You need to find a way to temper your enthusiasm and ambition. It's an ancient saying but true, Rome wasn't built in a day, and neither will your dream practice. Too many new owners begin implementing ambitious plans to improve the clinic's performance before the ink is dry on the sale agreement.

A better strategy is to focus on steadying the ship after the sale. Spend the first thirty days after taking over the practice getting to know your business, the finances, staff, patients, culture, and rhythms. Seek input from long-standing staff members and remember it takes a team to run a profitable practice. What works well? What would they change?

Make it a priority to sit down with the practice's accountant and get them to go through all the clinic's financial transactions with you. It is imperative you fully understand where you stand concerning revenue, expenses, and cash flow.

One of the best antidotes to those rose-tinted glasses is having a mentor who is not afraid to tell you the truth and point out your weaknesses.

Assembling Your Transition Team

Purchasing a dental practice is complicated. Just as a ship captain needs a harbor pilot to help guide them safely into port, you require a few seasoned professionals to help prevent you from making a costly mistake.

These professionals should have expertise in dental practice transitions. If you don't feel confident that your current accountant or lawyer has the necessary experience, then don't compromise—hire a transition expert. Remember, you have to get the practice purchase right the first time. It is a significant financial investment, and your first mistake could be your last. Inexperienced advisors can cost you money and maybe even the deal.

When anyone on a seller's transition team encounters advisors with little experience, they will take it as a sign that they can be more aggressive in furthering their client's best interests. Exploiting this weakness almost always ends up getting their clients a better deal.

We all know that first impressions count. When you enter your first negotiation session with a selling dentist they are likely to judge you by the professional company you keep. Having a heavyweight (i.e., an experienced transition specialist, a seasoned dental CPA, or a lawyer specializing in handling dental practice purchases) on your team will send a message that you may be younger and less experienced at dentistry than them, but you are not there to play games. Let the bargaining begin.

I can't stress enough the importance of having your team in place well before purchasing a practice. I have seen many dentists gather a team only after negotiations have gone off the rails, and the fact that they were then fighting a rearguard action was highly detrimental to their eventual deal.

When selecting your professional team, look for personal recommendations. Make a list of at least three candidates for each spot on your team. Conduct interviews with each person and ask about their particular experience in practice transitions. Don't be afraid to ask questions and discuss your expectations.

You should seek advisors who have a good grasp of dentistry and the unique issues you face. Hiring advisors with expertise in dental practice transitions will ensure that you get the best advice and prompt service. It's a small market; experienced advisors will have many dental clients and are motivated to maintain their reputation in the dental community.

Get to know your team of professionals, and never forget that while these professionals offer advice, the buck stops with you. It's your buck; and it is up to you to make the final decisions.

The Accountant

Look for an accountant to not only have experience with dentistry clients, but also some entrepreneurial acumen. You need them to give you proactive advice in structuring the proposed purchase. Expect your accountant to be involved in the following:

- ☐ Analyzing the vendor's financial statements.
- ☐ Preparing cash flow projections to ensure that the expected cash flow covers practice expenses, loan repayments, and your living expenses.
- ☐ Structuring the purchase in a way that achieves the best tax advantage.
- ☐ Assisting with arranging to finance the purchase.

The Lawyer

As with other members of your transition team, try to engage a lawyer familiar with handling the purchase and sale of dental practices. The tasks for your lawyer should include:

- ☐ Reviewing existing contractual arrangements.
- ☐ Analyzing the premise's lease to ensure the lease is assigned to you.
- ☐ Preparing the legal agreements and obtaining representations (before the closing date) to protect you against future claims.

The Dental Practice Acquisition Expert

The acquisition expert is the quarterback on your team. You should expect your transition expert to take a business approach to your proposed practice purchase: practical, no-nonsense, creative, and cost-efficient.

The transition expert is responsible for:

- ☐ Helping you find the most suitable practice.
- ☐ Giving you a realistic projection of future revenues and cash flow.
- ☐ Reviewing the vendor's practice valuation.
- ☐ Putting the dental practice *on the hoist* and checking for defects.
- ☐ Leading purchase negotiations.
- ☐ Preparing the initial letter of intent.
- ☐ Assisting legal counsel as required.
- ☐ Coordinating the services of outside advisors.
- ☐ Assisting in arranging financing.
- ☐ Structuring the business arrangement for the purchaser in multi-practitioner relationships.

When hiring a practice transition expert ask the following questions:

- ☐ How many years have you been in the transition business?
- ☐ How many practice transitions have you handled within the last five years?
- ☐ How do you charge for your services?
- ☐ Why should I choose you over your competitors?

Transition professionals know that any proposed transaction will only be successful if the financial and tax benefits are maximized for both the buyer and the seller. They are working in your best interests and worth the investment you make in them.

Key Takeaways

- ☐ Find the right clinic for you the first time; there are no do-overs.
- ☐ Owning a clinic is like owning a dog; it's a long-term commitment that requires constant attention.
- ☐ Be 100% sure that owning a dental practice fits your personal and professional goals, aspirations, and capabilities.

☐ Owning a dental practice means managing a clinic; it requires leadership.

☐ Practice ownership is an excellent investment, but the financial exposure of ownership is not for everyone.

☐ Be confident you can handle the pressure of meeting your monthly financial obligations. Don't get into arrears with the bank, or you face the prospect of them shutting you down.

☐ Build a team of capable advisors knowledgeable about dental transitions to assist in the purchase. Inexperienced advisors can cost you money and maybe even the deal.

☐ Get your spouse onside, especially concerning location.

☐ Use a short-term associateship to hone your clinical and patient communication skills and learn as much as you can about how a clinic should be managed. However, enjoy the benefits of ownership as soon as is feasible. Don't wait too long.

☐ The financial benefit of taking the early practice ownership route is significant. Many practice owners generate more than twice as much income as that of an associate.

☐ It is better to overpay for a good practice than get a poor one for cheap.

2

Exploring Purchasing Opportunities

Many associates are eager to purchase their own practices—more than there are practices available for sale, unfortunately. I know associates that have been looking for five years or more. When demand is greater than supply, prices rise, and good dental practices often become the object of bidding wars. The result is that they sell for more than they are worth. The fly in the ointment is that if you are an associate, there is a lot of pressure to become master of your own destiny. Undoubtedly, there is a substantial lost-opportunity cost of not becoming a practice owner as soon as possible. The bottom line is that you can generate significantly greater income (as much as $20,000 per month) as an owner. Every year you remain an associate, you are flushing these potential earnings down the drain.

Watching the Listings

In my experience, if you are looking to purchase a decent practice you will have to do a lot more than just look at the professional practice listings. That's what everyone else is doing, and you don't want to be like everyone else, do you? Becoming the owner of the practice of your dreams will take initiative, dedication, and energy—you will need to be proactive. Unconvinced? Let me give you some examples of the dangers of relying on listings.

When supply is limited you will be tempted to make compromises that lead to dangerous waters. One of the most common compromises is to look outside of your geographic comfort zone. I had a client, let's call him Marty, who couldn't find a suitable practice for sale in the city in which he lived. He searched for a long time before coming across an interesting rural listing. The practice was in a beautiful, small village; it was charming and showed a net income of $500,000. It was about two hours from the nearest town. On the upside, there was no other dentist in the area, and the asking price was half of what it would be if it were in the city. He loved the outdoor life, and the income he could make was more than he could have imagined. He bought the practice, and all was idyllic—except, perhaps, for the drive back home every weekend to see his girlfriend.

Things went well for a while—and then he got married. In the beginning it was good, and his new wife moved to the village with him. However, the arrival of their first child changed everything; his wife insisted on moving back to the city—with or without him. True to her ultimatum, she moved back to the city, and Marty commuted every weekend. It was a strain; he missed his family. Eventually, he put the practice up for sale and waited... Despite solid revenues, excellent profit margins, fresh air and the scenic environment, the isolation was not of interest to associates looking for a practice. Of course, you can sell anything if the price is right, so eventually Marty sold at a bargain-basement price.

The moral of the story is that moving to a rural community is not for everyone. You have to be sure that it will suit you and your family. Everyone involved has to accept the longevity of your career commitment. Another factor, should you consider commuting from elsewhere to a small rural community, is that many patients will resent the fact that you parachute in to take their money but are not involved in community life.

The longer you are forced into a holding pattern as an associate, waiting for that perfect practice to present itself, the more your criteria will take a bashing. Emma had been an associate for three years, time was ticking, and she began seriously looking for a practice to buy. Her primary criteria were that it had $600,000 of revenues and that the clinic had a minimum of four operatories. After a year of looking, she showed me the details of a clinic in which she was interested. It was an old practice with three operatories. Annual revenues were $400,000 with a net income that would barely cover expenses and a small salary for Emma. She purchased the practice thinking she would bring the clinic back to life and make it profitable. Unfortunately, more patients left than joined the practice over the following two years, and revenues continued to spiral down. If she had come to me before making her decision I would have advised her to look at the history of the business. The previous owner had been unable to increase revenues for the twenty years they owned the practice, so what made her, a young associate, believe she could turn the tide? Like Marty, she gave up and unloaded the clinic at a loss, losing most of her investment. The buyer was another local dentist whose existing practice lease was not renewed. He got a bargain in that he didn't have to pay for any goodwill. He transferred his patients to the new location and got a bonus by taking on what remained of Emma's patient list.

The Entrepreneurial Alternative

For many associates, practice ownership is non-negotiable. They will check the listings for years, hoping to get lucky, never giving up on their dream. If I have scared the living daylights out of you, and you feel despondent, don't. There is another way to own a practice, and that is to start one from scratch. I imagine many readers, almost involuntarily, took a sharp intake of breath after reading that suggestion. For many associates it will be way out of their comfort zone. To others the thought might be nightmare-inducing. Starting a dental practice is a case of risk and reward. Sure, there are significant risks, especially if you don't do it right, but many young dentists who took the plunge and started their own clinic have been successful beyond their wildest expectations.

Here's a quick test: imagine spending every penny you have, borrowing to the maximum extent a bank will allow, investing in a ton of leasehold improvements and equipment, and then hiring a full complement of staff, all of whom are dependent on you for their livelihood. Now imagine the ribbon-cutting ceremony and a thriving practice. How do you feel? If you feel scared witless but intrigued and excited, then starting out on your own may well be worth investigating.

If you are sweating profusely and your hands are shaking, and all you can see is the ribbon fluttering to the ground as you look at an empty reception area without a patient in sight, then you may lack the entrepreneurial spirit you will need to take this route to ownership. And there is nothing wrong with that.

However, for those with an entrepreneurial drive, the combination of a highly visible retail location situated in a growing neighborhood of young families may be irresistible. If the clinic also has committed employees and is open on weekends and evenings, many young start-up dentists will likely exceed even their most optimistic income projections.

The Proactive Approach

By now you may be thinking that if watching the listings isn't the answer, and the entrepreneurial route sounds downright scary, what else can you do? Take the road less travelled; proactively target and approach dentists who may be considering retiring, slowing down, or taking on a partner.

Cold-calling dentists is the down-and-dirty approach to beating your competitors to a jewel of a practice. In my experience the 80/20 rule applies here. Only around twenty percent of practice sales come from broker's listings, while about eighty percent are handled privately.

Directly approaching owners is a lot more complicated than answering an advertisement, but it will give you a far greater chance of owning your own practice. With the direct approach, you can bypass competing with other associates fighting for the same opportunity.

Step One – Where do You Want to Work?

Define the geographic area you (and your spouse) are willing to consider. In most cases this will be close to where you currently live or within easy commuting distance. There is an advantage to working and living in the same geographic location. You are part of the community and will bump into your patients in the grocery store, at school events with your children, or simply walking the neighborhood. Patients like to see that you are invested in the community.

Of course, there is nothing to prevent you from taking the opportunity of buying a practice to move lock, stock, and barrel to your dream location. As I mentioned earlier, just be sure the rest of your family is as keen as you on the adventure.

Step Two – Create a Database

Research how many dental practices are working in your chosen neighborhoods. Given that we live in the age of Google, this is easy. A quick online search will bring them up, and all you need do is create a list of their contact data and other relevant information. Ensure you have each practice's website address since the next step involves a little innocent stalking!

Step Three – Identify Likely Candidates

Visit each website and click whatever link takes you to the clinic's team biographies. The first person listed is most often the owner. If the photograph is of an older person, it's a good sign they may be more open to at least considering the long-term future of their practice. Make notes of whatever information you can glean from their online bio: their achievements, hobbies, etc. These may come in handy as icebreakers during subsequent phone calls.

When looking to buy a practice, investigate as many opportunities as possible. Cast your net as wide as possible. Consider options that do not necessarily fit your specific criteria. The more buying opportunities you analyze, the more market insight you will gain. This will give you greater confidence and sharpen your negotiating skills when pursuing a particular option.

Use your research to refine your database and narrow it down to those practices that meet your criteria and whose owners best fit the profile of someone who might entertain the possibility of selling up sometime soon.

Step Four – Send an Introductory Letter

Here is where I recommend you go old school and write a letter outlining your interest in their practice. Include your resume containing relevant information regarding your education, clinical experience, licenses and professional memberships, your professional development, and some personal information such as your hobbies and other interests.

In addition, emphasize that the reason you are reaching out is to assist them in their practice transition should they be considering this in the near future. Be clear that this could be an outright sale or a transition from associate to owner over a period of time.

Request a short meeting at the person's office and say that you will be in contact. Perhaps give a date by which you will be in touch.

Here is an example of a basic introductory letter.

Dear Dr. Seller,

My name is Dr. Al Dente. After working for three years as an associate, I am now ready to pursue my goal of practice ownership.

If you are contemplating selling your practice in the foreseeable future, I would very much like to speak to you. I would also be interested in joining your practice as an associate with a future option to purchase.

As you can see from my enclosed resume, I have the qualifications, experience, and passion for providing your patients with the high level of care to which they have become accustomed.

I would be grateful if we could talk about how I can assist you in implementing your practice transition. To this end, I will call you next week to arrange a time.

I look forward to meeting with you.

Regards,

Dr. Al Dente

Step Five – First Meeting Preparation

Before the first contact, you need to ask yourself: what information do I need from the seller? What research do I need to undertake before I approach the potential seller?

The aim of the introductory letter is just that—to get you through the door for a meet and greet. It's wise to manage your expectations for the initial get-to-know-you meeting. Going in full-bore expecting to come out with a deal to purchase the practice is unrealistic. It will likely scare away a dentist who may only be in the early stages of considering selling or transitioning out of their practice.

When you speak to the owner remember that they are a dentist running a busy practice, and their time is limited. Ask how much time they can set aside for the meeting and plan your visit accordingly.

The initial meeting is all about first impressions. You will likely be dealing with an older person, so riding in on a skateboard might not be the best approach. Treat the owner with respect, dress appropriately for a business meeting, and act like a consummate professional. First impressions mean acknowledging the staff, making eye contact, offering a firm handshake, and reading the tenor of the meeting. The latter means reading the owner's body language and listening for clues as to how they want to proceed. For example, if they start looking at their watch, they are probably running out of time or simply feel the meeting has run its course. Alternatively, if they are keen to show you their newest technology, or introduce you to critical members of staff, then they may be happy to extend your visit. You may then be able to ask questions that would typically be more appropriate for a follow-up practice visit. Reading the room can pay dividends.

The best advice I can give you for this first meeting is to listen far more than you talk. Let the owner tell you all about their practice. They are almost certainly very proud of what they have achieved. You need to show your recognition by nodding or making short affirmative comments such as "that's great," "wow, that's impressive," "that's so interesting," etc. Remember, in any conversation, the person who speaks the most always feels that the conversation or meeting went better than the other person.

Ask open questions using who, what, when, where, why, and how. Your primary goals are to bond with the owner and gather as much information as possible from them. The more they tell you, the more likely they are bonding with you and considering you as a potential future owner. Look for clues as to when they might consider either retiring or beginning the transition process. For many dentists, their journey towards retirement can take a few years as they first ease back on their responsibilities, their patient load, and the number of days they work. Rome wasn't built in a day, and you will need a little patience. Your reward will be to have the owner on hand during the transition period. They will help you reduce the attrition rate when you eventually take over the practice. If you were to purchase a dental practice off the shelf, the dentist may want out immediately or in short order, which could test patient loyalty.

Here's a crib sheet of the crucial information you should be looking to get from your first meeting. What you don't discover organically during the initial meeting can become questions to ask at the follow-up meeting if one occurs.

☐ Are they giving any indication they are considering starting the transition into retirement?

☐ Have they considered bringing on an associate who will reduce their workload in the short term and who would eventually purchase the practice?

☐ Are they considering selling, and if so, for what reason? Do they have an exit strategy?

☐ Does the practice have an associate? Is the associate subject to a restrictive covenant?

☐ What is the estimated value of the practice?

☐ What is the annual production?

☐ What gross and net revenues does the practice enjoy?

☐ Is the practice growing? How many new patients does it see per month?

☐ How many active patients do they have? How many patients were seen in the last 18 months?

☐ What are the lease terms for the premises? Is there an option to purchase the building if they own the real estate?

☐ What is the staff profile (e.g., staff positions and years of service)?

☐ What is the treatment profile?

Many of the questions above will be left unanswered after the initial visit. Still, it is helpful to bear them in mind so you can squirrel nuggets of information away as they come out in conversation. After all, the fact that the owner was willing to meet you indicates there is some interest in exploring the possibility of a transition.

Step Six – The Practice Visit

Assuming your introductory letter worked and you attended an exploratory meeting with one or more practice owners—which went well— you are now going to head back for a more serious practice visit. Here's where things get serious, the gloves are off, and it's time to ask some pointed questions.

First, consider what pertinent information you need from the seller such as background information about the dentist and the practice. Second, consider what personal information you are willing to share with the seller.

Your goal should be to obtain sufficient information to determine whether each opportunity you identify is worth pursuing. Collect as much information as you can on the clinic's reputation. Assess the practice location as well; is it located in an area where you want to practice? Is the community economically stable? Is there real potential for growth?

When you set up the meeting ensure that you meet with the dentist alone, not with their entire entourage of accountant, lawyer, and transition specialist. If necessary, explain that you want to get to know them better before entering into more formal negotiations.

During this visit you'll want to judge how well your practice philosophies and personalities align. Differences in attitudes toward patients, staff, technology, and treatment plans are all on the table. If you don't warm to the dentist, walk away. If you don't see eye to eye with the owner, what chance do you think you will have with their patients and staff?

I have witnessed hundreds of transitions over the years and the hugely successful ones are those where the purchaser and the seller hit it off instantly. Being on the same page regarding ethics, values, principles, and overall practice philosophy will result in a smooth transition. Obstacles to the sale will be overcome, and the sales process will move quickly.

Revisit the questions from step five. If there are any left unanswered, add them to the following list of things you need to investigate during your practice visit.

1. What is the demographic breakdown of patients (age, location, etc.)?

2. What is the likelihood of the patients who don't live close to the practice leaving after the purchase?

3. How many patients have left the practice in the last two years, and why did they go?

4. What are the growth trends of the practice?

5. At what capacity is the practice running?

    a. Can it comfortably handle the existing patient volume—more?

6. How many operatories does the clinic have, and how many are used?

7. Could operatories be added without significant renovations?

8. What is the overall condition and appearance of the office?

   a. Is the facility in need of a facelift?

   b. How much would this cost?

9. Is there adequate parking for staff and patients?

10. Does the practice have a website?

    a. Does it need updating?

    b. Does it feature online booking?

11. Does the practice have a social media presence?

    a. If so, to what extent?

    b. How positive are the reviews?

12. Is the management structure appropriate for the size of the practice?

13. Is the practice fully staffed, understaffed, or overstaffed?

14. Is there a comprehensive policy and procedures manual (including policies on vacation time, sick time, overtime, salary increases, benefits, etc.)?

15. Does the practice carry out performance evaluations?

    a. If so, how often?

16. How do staff salaries compare to the industry average?

    a. On what criteria are salary increases based?

    b. When was the last round of salary increases?

    c. When are employees expecting their next increase?

    d. Do salary increases reflect employee productivity?

17. What employee changes will be required?

    a. What is the likelihood that some staff members will not stay after the purchase?

18. What renovations are required to improve efficiency?

19. Could the practice be relocated at a reasonable cost?

20. Is the office technology up-to-date?

    a. Is the equipment in good working order?

21. How optimized are the accounts receivable?

    a. Does the practice have a formal accounts receivable strategy?

    b. What is the clinic's bad-debt ratio?

22. Is the practice charging above the fee schedule?

23. What component of the total office production is the hygiene business?

    a. Is the hygiene component of the practice fully utilized?

    b. How many hygiene days are there per week?

24. What proportion of endodontics, periodontics, oral surgery, and implant placement is outsourced?

25. How many days does the owner take off per year?

26. Will the dentist assist with financing the purchase?

27. Does the dentist own the real estate?

    a. If so, is there a possibility of purchasing it?

    b. If not, is there a good lease in place?

    c. What are the basic features of the lease, including terms, renewal options, etc.?

Key Takeaways

☐ There is a limited inventory of dental practices for sale. You may need to look at other options (e.g., starting your own practice or becoming a partner).

☐ The longer you have to wait for the perfect practice to come up for sale, the more your purchase criteria will be compromised.

☐ Becoming the owner of the practice of your dreams will take initiative, dedication, and energy—you will need to be proactive in your search.

☐ Target and approach dentists who may be considering retiring, slowing down, or taking on a partner. Go old school and write them a letter.

- ☐ Investigate as many opportunities as you can, it will give you more insight into the market. Cast your net as wide as possible. Consider options that don't fit your specific criteria.

- ☐ Consider opportunities to transition from associate to owner over time.

- ☐ Approximately twenty percent of practice sales come from broker's listings, while about eighty percent are handled privately.

- ☐ If you can't find a suitable practice to buy, starting your own practice is a matter of risk and reward. It is not for everyone.

3

Investigating the Purchase Opportunity

Okay, you have a potential dental practice that is available for sale; maybe you are lucky enough to have a choice. What do you need to do next? My suggestion is to take a small step back and determine your purchase options. What is the seller's exit strategy, and does it meet your objectives? If at this point you are confused because you thought you were just going to hand over a ton of cash, get the keys to the clinic and start seeing patients, then you might want to examine the most common ways a sale of a dental practice unfolds.

Types of Sale

Straight Sale

The straight sale is the one you may have been thinking of; you hand over the cash in exchange for the keys to the clinic. It's just like a real estate deal. This type of sale is clean, straightforward, and you are in complete control. You might only see the seller if they come back to handle occasional retreatments. Depending on the situation you may ask the seller to stay on for a short period, on a part-time basis, to help you with the transition and introduce you to the patients.

Pros	Cons
Save paying associate fees to the seller	Potentially more patient attrition
All revenues belong to the buyer	Possible conflict with seller's leadership style
Avoids treatment-philosophy conflicts	Unable to consult on patient treatment

Seller/Associate Sale

In some cases, a dentist selling their practice may not be quitting dentistry. They are selling to relieve themselves of the headaches of managing a clinic. This is not uncommon, and you will find cases where the seller wants to remain as an associate for several years. There is nothing wrong with buying a practice under these conditions, but you will have to ensure there is enough work, and more importantly, growth potential to keep you and the seller busy.

In this situation you must analyze the practice's finances to ensure there is sufficient cash flow to service your purchase loan, pay the practice's overhead, and pay yourself enough to at least cover your living expenses.

One other thing to watch for is that you will have purchased the clinic's patient charts, but the seller will be maintaining a relationship with them. You have to question how challenging it will be to transition the patients to your list when the seller decides to leave.

Pros	Cons
No patient attrition	A reduced income for the initial years
More time for marketing to grow the practice	Possible incompatible practice philosophy
Little to no employee turnover	Some patient attrition when the seller leaves

Partnership Interest Sale

Instead of purchasing the dental assets directly, you buy an interest in a partnership. The partnership owns all the practice assets and employs the staff. If you buy 25% of the partnership, you own 25% of the partnership assets and are entitled to the same percentage of the partnership income. A key consideration in dental partnerships is that each partner receives income based on the clinical revenues produced by that partner. The partner receives a payment based on the percentage of their collections, minus laboratory expenses.

Partnership agreements are complex as they deal with many components of a partnership, including:

- [ ] A stipulated number of hours each partner agrees to work.

- [ ] Terms surrounding voluntary or mandatory withdrawal from the business.

- [ ] What happens when a partner retires.

- [ ] The role and responsibilities of the managing partner.

Pros	Cons
Better work-life balance	You may disagree with majority decisions
Financial risks are shared	Difficult to withdraw from the partnership
More income due to economies of scale	Less control of how the clinic is managed

Putting the Practice on the Hoist

Buying a clinic is a little like buying a car; you need to look under the hood, put the vehicle on a hoist and take a good look at the chassis and other moving parts. With a dental practice, your checklist should include: location, size, revenues, equipment, and anything else listed in your purchasing criteria.

The Practice Valuation

Your first question will be "is the asking price reasonable?" If you've been checking out dental practice listings for a while, you'll have a good idea of what a realistic price is, given your criteria. However, never take a practice valuation at face value; always get a professional opinion from a practice transition specialist—one who knows the market intimately. If they agree that the valuation is fair, your next step is due diligence. My advice? There is due diligence, and there is luck. If you decide to rely on luck, consider buying a lottery ticket, not a dental practice.

How do you do due diligence? First, dissect the valuation report. Your eye will be drawn to the practice's gross revenues—that nice fat number—but ignore that for a moment and look at how much you can take home every pay cycle. How large is the patient pool, how much has it brought in over the last year or two, and how much will it earn the clinic in the future? The critical thing to consider is whether enough patients are coming through the door to provide sufficient income to service your debt load, pay the practice's overhead, and for you to earn a decent living.

When assessing the equipment and the condition of the clinic, be sure to keep things in perspective. Don't get too hung up on the age of the equipment as long as it is functioning well. The same goes for a clinic that may require some TLC; remember, you can make allowances for capital expenditures when making your offer.

In practical terms, take a close look at the financial statements and projections. Remember, you are looking for the answer to the question that should be top of mind, "Is the cash flow sufficient to service my practice debt and pay for my living expenses?"

What should you look for? The first thing you ought to notice is that the practice's income statement, prepared by its accountant, is significantly different from the one the valuator has used to value the practice.

Surely they should be the same, right? In this case, you have to have your wits about you because the valuator adds back depreciation and discretionary expenses. The latter includes associate fees, promotional expenditure, automobile costs, equipment leases, and payments to family members. All these, and more, can be added back into income.

The question you have to ask is, "are all these things discretionary?" For instance, if family members are not working in or providing necessary services to the clinic, they can probably be classed as discretionary. But, if any of them are working in the clinic, even on a part-time basis, you will need to replace them with paid employees. Therefore, a reasonable salary amount needs to be returned to the expenses column to hire someone to carry out those duties.

Another cash flow adjustment is required when the seller owns the property. Often only the operating costs are expensed. You will need to ensure that an equitable amount for rent is added to the practice's operating costs.

When reviewing the practice's cash flow statement, ask yourself if the associate fee remains an expense or should be added back into income. Let's assume revenues are $1.2 million with $800,000 produced by the principal and the remaining $400,000 generated by the associate. The income statement shows an associate fee expense of $150,000, and you see that the valuator has added this expense back into income. In this case, the valuator assumes that an associate is not required to generate total revenues of $1.2 million.

Adding the associate fee of $150,000 into cash flow can increase the value of the practice by a substantial amount. So the decision of whether or not to add back the $150,000 of associate fees is a big deal. If you think that you can generate $1.2 million of revenues on your own, then you would accept the valuator's calculation. On the other hand, if you think you can only generate the same revenue as the principal, you must deduct the associate fees of $150,000 from the valuator's cash flow statement.

Never simply look at the current year's income statement. It rarely gives the complete picture. You will need to look back three to five years. A current year's income statement can look good when a dentist is retiring because they let their patients know they will be leaving. At that point the patients become motivated to complete their treatment plans.

My tip? Identify whether the valuator is basing the valuation solely on the current year, or are they considering the previous year's financial statements when calculating the practice's actual value?

It is vital that you and your bank base five year income projections on past growth patterns while at the same time considering the new initiatives you are going to implement to grow the practice.

Finding the Diamond in the Rough

Finding a great dental practice requires an open mind. In some cases, a clinic that's up for sale hides its real potential. So, how do you find a diamond in the rough? Be thorough and study the valuation reports. As you wade through the reports you will often come across a practice that seems like a contradiction. Some time ago I came across such an offering.

The practice was only three years old, in a dynamite location, and had new equipment. But its annual revenues were only $600,000 with a net operating cash flow of $200,000. My interest piqued, I questioned why this practice was doing so poorly.

The practice had languished on the market for a while, passed over by several young dentists looking for the perfect turnkey operation. The trouble with perfect, of course, is that there's a lot of competition, and that drives up the price.

I dug deeper. The valuation showed that the owner had two other practices and only worked in his newest practice for one day a week. Two part-time associates (recent graduates) split the other days between them. The clinic was state-of-the-art and featured all-new, top-of-the-line equipment.

It was a start-up starved of its owner's oxygen. It was doomed from the day it opened. A start-up needs the owner's total commitment to establish patient relationships and build the practice. Patients are less likely to commit to treatment plans when the proposal is presented by a young, recently graduated associate.

An entrepreneurial young dentist spotted the potential of this particular practice. She studied the valuation report and saw what *could be*, not what *was*. She purchased the clinic despite her accountant's objections. He was concerned about the practice's current financial position. Within one year, revenues broke $1 million and continue to grow. I saw her recently, and she still can't believe her good fortune in getting such a bargain.

Never underestimate the value of studying a valuation report.

The Break-Even Analysis: An Indispensable Tool in Finding an Excellent Practice

A break-even analysis is like a depth finder on a boat—it tells you how close you are to running aground. Put another way, it shows you how far the revenues of the practice you're considering purchasing can drop before hitting rock-bottom. In this case, rock-bottom is the moment net revenues only cover the practice's expenses. Depth finders help mariners navigate away from dangerous waters; the break-even analysis will help you do the same, even before you get in the boat!

First, you need to ask, "what is the break-even revenue, and how do I calculate it?

Break-even revenue means that the revenue generated by the clinic matches that of the fixed and variable expenses.

Fixed expenses are those that don't change when revenues increase or decrease. Let's assume, based on the valuation report of the target clinic, you determine that the annual fixed expenses are $450,000. In this case, costs are $250,000 for clinic overhead, $80,000 for servicing the purchase loan, and a minimum of $120,000 for your living expenses.

The **variable** expenses are 15% of revenues and consist of dental supplies and lab fees, which are 7% and 8% of revenues, respectively. The remaining 85% of revenues contribute to paying for the fixed expenses. Accountants call the 85% the **Contribution Margin Percentage.**

To calculate the break-even revenue, divide the fixed expenses by the Contribution Margin Percentage. Break-even point = fixed expenses ÷ Contribution Margin Percentage.

In the above example the break-even point = $450,000 ÷ .85 = $529,412.

If the clinic brings in $530,000 in revenues it will pay for all the running costs, but there is virtually zero profit. In this case, where do you find the funds to upgrade the website, replace dental equipment, or take an extra draw to take your family on a Disney Caribbean cruise?

In dollars and cents, the break-even analysis provides the answer to whether or not you should consider buying the clinic. Unless future income projections indicate a substantial increase in revenues, the break-even analysis in the example above shows that you should move on to the next purchase opportunity.

The break-even calculation is essential when shopping for a dental practice and as a monthly management tool to monitor profitability. Like the depth finder mentioned earlier, it can alert you if you get too close to rock-bottom, so you can take immediate corrective action.

Location

The ideal location for a clinic is one with high visibility. You want to have maximum exposure to people during their daily commute or shopping. An attractive clinic with good street appeal is a patient magnet.

Beware of the clinic hidden on the third floor of a medical or commercial building. There are a lot of older practices for sale that are in locations that are not visible from the street. In the past there was a shortage of dentists; demand was high, and clinics were booked solid. This meant clinics could be located just about anywhere. In today's market, you cannot rely on new patients seeking you out. Sure, you might be okay for a while, but as soon as a new clinic opens in a retail environment with street exposure, your new patient will drop significantly.

Remember, expect attrition; people move, die, or change dentists on a whim. When assessing the value of a dental practice, check the attrition rate to know exactly how many new patients you need to attract every month to keep the practice stable, then look at the potential to grow the practice. If it is in a commercial building, could the other tenants and their employees offer a pool of new patients? Do the companies attract a lot of customers that would see your clinic? Check whether the building is accessible after hours and on weekends. Is there potential for expanding the space? What would that look like?

Demographics

Consider the neighborhood location of any practice you are investigating. Demographics are more critical than you might think at first. If the clinic is in an older neighborhood with little to no growth in the previous ten years, you should question how you will attract new clients from further afield. On the other hand, a neighborhood with new residential developments means new families moving to the area and a definite uptick in patients.

Call in at the local city or town hall and ask for information. Almost all towns and cities have information on their local population, including age, household income, population growth forecast, the levels of in-migrants arriving from other parts of the country, and immigrants moving from outside the country to the locale.

It's also a good idea to compare your area's population/dentist ratio with other locations to get a sense of the competition you will be facing. Then, check out your immediate competitors. How do they compare regarding office hours, social media presence, marketing, and community involvement?

Patient Information

In any transaction, knowledge is power. Discover as much as possible about the practice's patient base.

- [ ] Its total number of patients.
- [ ] The number of patients treated in the previous twelve months.
- [ ] The number of new patients per month (last twelve months).
- [ ] The age breakdown of patients.
- [ ] The percentage of patients not living within fifteen miles of the practice.

Treat the list above as a starting point. Depending on your location, different—or additional—patient information might be helpful.

Type of Work

Take a close look at the dental work being undertaken by the practice. You will quickly identify if the clinic focuses on basic dentistry or whether it carries out a significant amount of full mouth restorations. You are looking for an opportunity to increase revenues by offering more high-end treatments.

Facility Lease

Before you sign on the dotted line to purchase a dental practice, ensure you have an undisturbed tenancy agreement for ten to fifteen years. If the practice you are keen on has less than ten years on its lease, then inquire if the landlord is open to extending the lease. One thing to be very cautious of is a demolition clause. In my opinion this is a deal-breaker; it allows the landlord to terminate your lease if they decide to demolish the building. You have no security.

Team Profile

Your success in the practice will depend mainly on the quality of the team you inherit. It will be up to your employees to successfully transfer the practice's goodwill to you as the new dentist. You can determine how long employees have worked in the clinic from the valuation report and also assess their respective remuneration.

Management Information System

How is management measuring the practice's performance? Does it have a monitoring system to track overhead, treatment acceptance rate, dentist and hygiene productivity, conversions of inquiries into appointments, and new patient count? If it does, it is likely to be well-managed. If not, you will need to dig deeper to find the data you need to help make your decision. Also, be aware that you will have to implement this shortly after purchasing the practice, and train someone to collect and manage the data.

SWOT Analysis

A SWOT analysis is a strategic planning method that will surprise you with its simplicity and effectiveness if you have never used it before. It is something you can use to assess and compare purchase opportunities. Later, it will also help you plan for the future. The acronym stands for Strengths, Weaknesses, Opportunities, and Threats. To carry out a SWOT analysis, create a table with four columns, each headed with one of the terms. Then, with your advisory team, look at each column in turn and make a list of things that apply.

Here is an example.

STRENGTHS

- There has been a steady increase in annual revenues
- Overhead is lower than the industry average
- Good street exposure
- Ample patient parking

WEAKNESSES

- Website is outdated
- Marketing is non-existent
- Financial information is not current
- Basic dentistry only
- Three-month wait to see the doctor
- Only open to 5 pm, five days a week

OPPORTUNITIES

- Implement a management information system
- Update website and social media
- Develop marketing plan
- Increase high-end procedures
- Expand office hours

THREATS

- Stagnant local population
- New dental clinic moving next door
- Difficult to recruit staff
- Staff resistant to internal management changes

Once you have completed your SWOT analysis, refer to it continually as you start to build the practice. It will help keep your feet firmly on the ground as you plan the future of your business.

Key Takeaways

☐ A straight sale is similar to a real estate deal. You pay the agreed price, get the keys to the clinic, and you are in complete control.

☐ In a seller/associate sale deal, the selling dentist remains as an associate. Ensure there is enough work for both dentists and growth potential.

☐ In a partnership interest deal, the partnership owns the practice's assets. A key consideration is that each partner receives income based on the clinical revenues produced by that partner. Partnership agreements are complex.

☐ Take practice valuations at face value. Get a professional opinion from a practice transition specialist who knows the market intimately.

☐ Carry out due diligence on any potential purchase.

☐ The big question is: "Is there sufficient cash flow to service my practice debt and pay for my living expenses?"

☐ At a minimum, review the last three years' income statements. Identify whether the valuator based the valuation solely on the current year or considered the previous year's financial statements when calculating the practice's actual value.

☐ Never underestimate the value of studying a valuation report.

☐ The break-even analysis is an indispensable tool in finding an excellent dental practice.

☐ Remember the real estate maxim: location, location, location.

4

The Letter of Intent (LOI)

Before you can send the seller a letter of intent, you need to come up with a purchase price. This calculation can be challenging, particularly in urban areas experiencing a strong seller's market, where numerous buyers chase limited opportunities.

Case Study: Melissa

Let's follow Melissa's trials and tribulations. She has been an associate for five years and has searched for the perfect practice for two years. Caught in a seller's market for a long time, she is frustrated. She just received a valuation report for a new listing and is reviewing it over a latte in her local coffee shop. Her first impressions are positive; the clinic is the right size, in a good location, and has sufficient cash flow. It meets all her initial search criteria. The valuation has come in at $1 million, so that's the assumed asking price. That's all well and good, but what should she offer?

Let's join her in the coffee shop. As Melissa sips her coffee, she recalls the first time she tried to buy a dental practice; she was late submitting the offer and missed out on a great opportunity. She'd learned the hard way that good clinics sell fast. Even so, her last two on-time purchase offers had not been high enough to secure the clinics she wanted.

She feels a blast of chill air as the coffee shop door opens, and she looks up to see her transition expert, Robert, enter. He scans the room, smiles, and nods at the counter to see if she wants another drink. She nods and mouths, "Latte please."

A few minutes later he sits next to her, and after a few pleasantries, he pulls out his copy of the valuation. He has become her trusted advisor and tells her that after reviewing the report, he feels that based on current cash flow and slow historical growth, the practice is only worth $900,000. Melissa nods; it was what she expected. She also knows that what it's worth and what it will sell for are two different things entirely. At precisely the same time they say, "It'll go for more!" She knows there will be multiple offers, but it's at the top end of her financial comfort zone. She says, "Robert, perhaps I should offer $950,000?" Robert's answer is non-committal as he flips through the report. Second-guessing herself, she recalls a dentist friend with a very successful practice, who told her that he had almost lost out on buying his clinic because he began haggling over $50,000. She tells Robert the story, and they discuss the pros and cons of offering more. In the end, she decides to put an offer in for $1 million.

A few days later, she receives news that the seller had received multiple offers over $1 million. He is now offering all prospective buyers the opportunity to bid on the practice, and will accept the highest offer. A bidding war is not a good scenario; the clinic is in a good location, but it's still only an average clinic with four operatories and slow growth. In the end Melissa lost out; the clinic sold for $1.2 million, a cool $300,000 above what her transition expert felt it was worth. I regularly remind my clients that they have a purchasing budget for a good reason. I jokingly tell them that they are not the former Qatari prime minister who, in 2015, reportedly paid a whopping $179.4 million for Picasso's *Les Femmes d' Alger* at auction. At the time, it smashed the record for the most expensive artwork ever sold at the auction by $37 million.

If Melissa had got caught up in a bidding war and paid $300,000 more than the practice was worth, she would have had to service that additional practice debt. Always calculate ahead of time whether you can afford to bid more than you originally budgeted, and consider how that will impact your bottom line.

Like many associates, Melissa has struggled to find an urban practice that she can afford. What is the answer to her problem? It may not be her preferred option, but choosing to buy a clinic in a rural area would likely give her more options and more bargaining power. Of course, there is always a downside; rural practices may be easier to buy, but when the time comes to sell, they will more difficult to sell without making some concessions to potential buyers.

Case Study: Steven

Steven is an associate with four years of experience. When he began looking for a clinic in a rural area he'd expected to see a market with less competition and lower prices, giving him more bargaining power, but that hasn't been

Chapter 4: The Letter of Intent (LOI)

the case. Steven grew up on a farm, but he now works in a city practice. He missed the country life and decided to move back, purchase a rural clinic, and have a hobby farm. A clinic located in a dream area came across his desk. The listing price was $800,00, and the real estate was also available. The dental practice had been listed for over a year. Although there had been some interest, it had received no offers. Thinking he might be able to get a bargain, he submitted an offer of $650,000. The seller countered with a firm $750,000. In the end, Steven accepted the counter. It was less about the money and more about falling in love with the clinic and the location. He had assumed he could get a bargain by buying a rural clinic, but there are no guarantees that you will pay less just because the dental practice is not in a city.

The Real Estate Question

Dentists often ask me whether they should buy the real estate if it's available. It's a no-brainer; if it is at all feasible, you should always purchase the property. Horror stories abound about how seller-landlords can repossess the premises. These include not being able to renew the lease, triggering a demolition clause, or assigning the lease to another dentist. In some cases a buyer is kicked out onto the street, only to see the seller reinstall themselves as the practicing dentist and—in essence—repossess the clinic's assets, including leasehold improvements, equipment, and the lion's share of the goodwill.

Given the potential dangers of not owning the real estate, buyers are often willing to invest in purchasing the property. If the seller owns the real estate, buyers may either negotiate a long-term lease or make an offer to buy the property. The purchase price is usually based on the appraised value. If the purchase of both the practice and the real estate is too great a financial commitment, the buyer might ask the seller to grant an option to buy the real estate in the future when their bank is more amenable to help finance the property. Alternatively, the seller can give the buyer right of first refusal.

In my opinion, if the seller is stubborn and insists on retaining the real estate as a source of retirement income, I would advise passing on the opportunity. Even with an iron-clad, long-term lease, there is no guarantee you can stay as long as you want and be in a position to sell the clinic to a successor in twenty years. Leasing from the seller of a dental practice can be like a nagging toothache.

Now that we've seen some of the challenges surrounding the purchase price, let's take a closer look at the letter of intent.

Overview

- ☐ The LOI is the start, not the end, of the negotiations. The LOI is based on the valuation, and due diligence is only carried out after the terms of the LOI are accepted. The results of your inquiries and review of the records will often change the terms of the deal.

- ☐ The LOI is non-binding. Only after the removal of the purchase conditions will the LOI become binding.

- ☐ The LOI should be submitted as quickly as possible to avoid another offer being accepted ahead of yours. Once another offer is accepted, your offer will not be considered until the competing buyer fails to remove their conditions in a timely fashion.

- ☐ The LOI should be concise and written in plain English. The seller should not need a lawyer to translate the document.

- ☐ Keep the time between the date you submit the offer and the date you require an answer as short as possible. Limiting the time will prevent the seller from shopping your offer around for a higher price.

Composition of the Letter of Intent

A letter of intent is not binding on the buyer, except concerning confidentiality and exclusivity. The buyer is obligated to keep all information obtained about the seller's practice during negotiations strictly confidential. The only exclusions to this are professional advisors and other parties such as a bank, and even then only as necessary to pursue the completion of the purchase. In terms of exclusivity, the seller agrees not to negotiate with other parties with respect to the sale of the clinic until the conditions of the offer are satisfied (by the agreed date). Only if and when the conditions are not met, the offer is rescinded, or the LOI expires, is the seller free to negotiate with other buyers. The component parts of an LOI are discussed below.

The Purchase Price

The LOI stipulates the purchase price and whether it is an asset or stock deal. The former is where the buyer purchases the assets and liabilities (the sum of all assets less the sum of agreed liabilities) of the business. A stock deal is where the buyer buys the seller's stock in the corporation which owns the practice assets. You will need to talk to your accountant before deciding which route is more beneficial to your circumstances. Much will depend on what makes sense for both you and the seller. If you disagree, it will become a significant factor in the negotiation of the sale.

The purchase price is paid in cash on the agreed closing date. If a buyer does not receive bank financing for the total amount of the purchase price, they can potentially ask that the seller finance the remaining portion of the purchase price. In this case, on the closing date the seller would receive the purchase price comprised of cash and a promissory note from the buyer.

On larger dental practice purchases, buyers sometimes ask for a part of the purchase price to be considered an earn-out. An earn-out is where the buyer retains a portion of the agreed sale price and pays it out to the seller over time. However, post-sale, the seller will be required to meet certain conditions in maintaining revenues at a stipulated level. A seller will usually only consider an earn-out arrangement if the deal offers them more money than they might receive from another buyer. As part of this type of deal, the seller works as an associate during the earn-out period. The advantage to the buyer is that they are sharing the risks of future revenues with the seller.

It should be noted that sellers are not in the financing business and will only consider creative financing options if no potential buyers offer a cash deal.

The Deposit

The deposit, or earnest money, is payable shortly after the letter of intent is accepted. The funds will be held in trust either by the buyer's broker or lawyer. Often, the buyer is required to increase the deposit once the purchase conditions are removed and the deal becomes binding.

The List of Assets

The purchase typically includes the following assets:

a. The leasehold improvements and fixtures.

b. Office furniture, equipment computers, hand instruments, handpieces, etc.

c. All inventory and supplies, at approximately the same levels as maintained in the ordinary course of business.

d. The goodwill of the dental practice, including all patient lists and patient records, financial records, x-rays and models, the existing telephone numbers and fax numbers, social media accounts, websites, email addresses, and trade names.

Certain assets will be excluded, including:

a.   Accounts receivable and cash on hand.

b.   Any personal mementos, including textbooks and artwork.

Accounts Receivable

The buyer often collects the accounts receivable on behalf of the seller for a specified time after the sale and remits the receipts less a management fee, usually 5 percent. Alternatively, the buyer requests to buy the accounts receivable. The purchase price is often adjusted to reduce the exposure of uncollected receivables and account for potential bad debts. The reason for purchasing the receivables is that it provides immediate working capital to the buyer.

The Closing Date

In most cases, the closing date is set between sixty and ninety days after the LOI is signed. Sometimes the buyer or seller requests to delay the closing date because of holidays or a delayed moving date for the buyer. In my experience, if the time between the initial signing of the letter of intent and the closing date is four months or longer, the greater the chance that the deal will not be completed. If the buyer requests an extension to the closing date, the seller will likely increase the deposit as an additional security measure. In all cases, the amount owing needs to be paid by the closing date as laid out in the purchase agreement.

Non-Competition/Non-Solicitation

This clause prevents the seller from:

- ☐ Practicing dentistry within a specific geographic radius of the practice for an agreed number of years.
- ☐ Soliciting employees of the practice for an agreed number of years.
- ☐ Soliciting patients of the practice at any time.

Associateship

It is vital that the seller remains in the dental practice for a period to ease the transition. As early as possible, inform the seller what your expectations are regarding their associateship. For instance, a typical clause in the letter of intent might read, "The seller will work as an associate for two days per week for three months. After related laboratory fees, the remuneration will be 40 percent of collections. The buyer can terminate the associateship at any time with two weeks' notice. The parties will mutually agree on the days worked."

Conditions Precedent

Here is a sample of typical conditions for the buyer's benefit.

a. On or before (date), the buyer will have arranged adequate financing.

b. On or before (date), the buyer will have reviewed and approved the practice's financial statements and other financial information.

c. On or before (date), the buyer will have completed the patient chart audit.

d. On or before (date), the buyer will have reviewed and accepted the lease agreement for the premises.

e. On or before (date), the buyer will have entered into an agreement to purchase the property in which the premises are situated.

f. On or before (date), they have examined and been satisfied with the inspection of the dental equipment of the practice.

g. On or before (date), buyer and seller will have entered into a purchase agreement.

Patient Retreatment Clause

As long as the seller is still an associate of the practice, they are responsible for any retreatments on patients seen before the closing date. Once the seller is no longer an associate, if any retreatments are required, it will be at the buyer's discretion to perform the retreatment at no cost to the seller, or to refer the patient to the seller for treatment.

Employees

Until the closing date, the seller will not alter the terms and conditions of employment of any practice employee without the buyer's prior approval.

Transition

The seller agrees to do everything possible to ensure the effective transfer of the practice's goodwill to the buyer, including signing a mutually acceptable letter of introduction, which the buyer may send to the practice's patients.

The seller will not send any letters to the clinic's patients without the buyer's prior consent. In addition, the seller will make themselves available (within reason) for a period after the closing date to address any questions the buyer may have concerning the practice, including information regarding particular patient histories, dental equipment, or staffing issues.

Due Diligence

Once the seller signs the letter of intent you can proceed with a detailed investigation (due diligence) of the practice's business. Due diligence ensures that you receive what was agreed upon. This process will uncover any skeletons in the seller's closet.

Key Takeaways

- ☐ Know your purchasing budget and stick to it. Bidding wars lead to servicing a larger practice debt.

- ☐ If it is at all feasible, always purchase the property.

- ☐ If the seller insists on retaining the real estate as a long-term source of retirement income, pass on buying the practice.

- ☐ The letter of intent (LOI) is the start, not the end, of the negotiations; it is non-binding.

- ☐ Submit your LOI as quickly as possible and write it in plain English. Keep the time between the submission date and the date you require an answer as short as possible.

- ☐ The LOI stipulates the purchase price and whether it is an asset or stock deal.

- ☐ A deposit is paid shortly after the LOI is accepted.

- ☐ The closing date is usually between sixty and ninety days after signing the LOI.

- ☐ Determine if there is a benefit for the seller to remain in the dental practice for a period of time to ease the transition.

CHAPTER

5

Due Diligence

Once your letter of intent is accepted you take control of the *potential* transition. I say potential because you have a lot of work to do to ensure that everything is as it seems and now that you can look under the hood of the practice, you still want to make the purchase.

Case Study: Jordan

Jordan recently submitted an offer to a dentist's broker to purchase a clinic. Both Jordan and the seller have a transition consultant on their team, and Jordan's consultant Glenn just called to tell him that, although there were four other bidders, Jordan's was the highest. Although he is excited and tempted to get the *special occasion* bottle of champagne from the fridge, he realizes that this is not the end of the transition process; it is just the beginning. Up to this point, the seller controlled everything; now, it is his turn to discover whether the dental practice is worth the sticker price. Jordan is fortunate that he has Glenn, a very experienced transition specialist, on his team to carry out the due diligence audit on the practice. Jordan recalls Glenn tapping the side of their nose and saying, "Don't worry, I know where the bodies are buried."

Up to this point, the seller has been in the background. The dentist wasn't at the clinic when Jordan's broker took him on an after-hours tour. He hasn't met the dentist, nor any of the staff. The first step, therefore, is to go and meet the seller. He wants to ensure that they connect personally and professionally and that their practice philosophies align.

Jordan's friend Patty bought a practice a while ago despite not getting along with the outgoing dentist and disagreeing with how he ran his practice. There were multiple challenges with the sale; she and the seller argued over just about everything. Then, when she eventually took over, she realized the seller's practice philosophy hung over the practice like a bad smell. The employees had become used to his way of working and butted against Patty's new, more modern, approach to running the clinic. Even some of the patients wanted her to do things "Dr. Smith's way."

Glenn had told Jordan at their first meeting that the most successful transitions occur when buyer and seller hit it off instantly. When two people share the same philosophy and values, the transition is smooth, and any obstacles in the purchase and sale process are quickly removed. His advice stuck with Jordan, "If you have trouble bonding with the dentist on your first visit, make it your last."

A few days later, Jordan meets with Glenn to review the key issues they need to address before beginning a full due diligence audit. The first thing Glenn points out is that the valuation report did not address **lease renewal**. He suggests that the lease term plus renewal options should be at least fifteen years. This period of time will allow Jordan to repay the purchase debt comfortably and accrue sufficient savings for capital expenditures and personal expenses. Glenn emphasizes the importance of having an undisturbed tenancy for the length of the lease, including renewal options. Undisturbed tenancy means there must be no demolition or relocation clauses in the lease.

Glenn notes that the clinic has a long-term associate. He advises Jordan to ensure there is a cast-iron **restrictive covenant** in the associate's agreement. This covenant would prevent them from setting up independently or at another clinic and luring away patients and employees. Jordan says, "But surely all associates sign one of those things, don't they? I know I had to; I was even given a bonus to sign." Glenn shakes his head, "Jordan, you can't take anything for granted. Associates know they have a lot more leverage if they avoid signing a restrictive covenant, so some hold out."

Next on the agenda for pre-due diligence talks with the seller is whether they will **stay on after the sale** to help the transition and introduce patients. Glenn tells Jordan that it's a good idea to have the dentist hang around for maybe two days a week, but for no longer than six months. A greater number of days or a more extended period of time can cause serious problems. A good analogy for this scenario is that the seller has sold the cow but has kept the milk. If a selling dentist works too many hours, it is unlikely there will be enough practice income to pay the buyer's living expenses and loan repayments. In my opinion, this is a deal killer.

Finally, Glenn points to the **employee profile** in the valuation report. "Jordan, this could be an issue. You will need to have a serious conversation with the seller about staffing and salaries." Jordan looks up from the report, expecting more, and Glenn explains what he sees as the challenges. The clinic, which has been open for thirty years, has two hygienists who have been there for more than twenty years. To keep them from leaving, the dentist has steadily increased their salaries over the years to the point they are earning significantly more than the industry average. The other three staff members, a receptionist and two assistants, have worked at the clinic for less than eighteen months. The first challenge lies in the relationship patients have with the hygienists. If they were to leave, how many patients would follow them? In this case, Jordan would have to carry on paying over the odds if he wanted them to stay, and even then, that offers no guarantees. Glenn notes that the clinic's revenue has been stagnant for the previous few years. In its current situation, it couldn't absorb losing too many patients. The second challenge Glenn sees is that the clinic may be suffering from low office morale, given that sixty percent of the employees have been there for less than eighteen months.

Jordan looks up from his notes, "Wow, Glenn, this employee stuff seems like a nasty can of worms. How the heck can I protect myself?" Glenn explains that they could negotiate a holdback from the proceeds of the sale. The seller would receive the holdback once the hygienists had remained at the practice for a set period. "You have to remember, Jordan, that you are paying a large sum of money in expectation of achieving clinic revenues in line with past performance. If two revenue-earning employees take patients away shortly after you take over, then the clinic is not worth what you paid."

In Jordan's case, he and his transition expert identified four deal-breakers that needed to be dealt with before he spent time doing full due diligence. Once you have determined your deal-breakers, walk away from the deal if you don't receive a satisfactory answer from the seller.

Assuming all your deal-breakers are satisfactorily resolved, you can proceed with the due diligence audit. I'll give you a breakdown of a simple audit—but each transition is unique, so you may need to add a few procedures of your own. While you work on the audit, retain the services of a dental equipment specialist to report on the age and condition of the clinic's equipment and advise on what maintenance or repairs are required.

Due Diligence Audit

Financial Review

- ☐ Ask your CPA (choose one with experience in dental practices) to obtain copies of the tax returns and financial statements for the clinic's previous four years. Use these to identify revenue and expense trends.

- ☐ Ask your CPA to prepare cash flow projections and recommendations regarding reducing clinic overhead.

Patients

- ☐ Review a representative sample of the clinic's patient charts to get an idea of the quality of patient care, the type of dental treatments performed, any remaining treatments, patient needs, and any areas where you might increase revenues.

- ☐ Is the seller's treatment philosophy compatible with your own?

- ☐ How does the practice monitor treatment acceptance?

- ☐ How many active patients does the clinic have, and what is its definition of *active*?

- ☐ What are the demographic characteristics of the patients (i.e., age, income, and location)?

- ☐ On average, how close do patients live to the dental clinic?

  - ☐ What is the likelihood that patients who don't live close to the clinic will move to a different practice after the purchase?

- ☐ How many patients have left the practice in the last two years?

  - ☐ For what reasons did they leave?

- ☐ How many inactive patients does the clinic list?

  - ☐ What procedures are in place to reactivate these patients?

- ☐ What is the clinic's fee structure, and is there leeway to generate more revenues?

- ☐ Where do new patients come from: referrals, advertising, social media?

Employees

- ☐ What is the salary of each staff member?

- [ ] Are you willing and able to maintain current salaries?
- [ ] Are salaries comparable to the industry average?
- [ ] On what criteria have salary increases been decided?
- [ ] When was the last round of salary increases?
- [ ] When is the staff expecting another increase?
- [ ] Is on-the-job performance evaluated?
  - [ ] How often?
  - [ ] Do salary increases reflect employee productivity? If not, why not?
- [ ] Do you consider the practice understaffed or overstaffed?
  - [ ] Would you consider hiring more employees or working with fewer employees?
- [ ] Is there a policy and procedures manual?
- [ ] Does the practice maintain professional personnel files?
- [ ] Is the management structure appropriate for the size of the practice?

Facility

- [ ] Is the clinic working at, under, or over capacity?
  - [ ] How does it handle current patient volumes?
  - [ ] How many operatories are in use?
  - [ ] Can operatories be added without a major renovation?
  - [ ] What renovations are required to improve efficiency?
- [ ] What is the overall condition and appearance of the clinic?
  - [ ] Is the facility in need of a facelift?
  - [ ] Is work required immediately?
- [ ] Is there adequate parking for staff and patients?
- [ ] Has your legal counsel reviewed the terms and conditions of the lease?
  - [ ] What are their recommendations?
- [ ] What are the clinic's operating hours?
  - [ ] Could office hours be expanded to include evenings and weekends?

Equipment

- ☐ Compare the equipment listed in the valuation report with what you see during your clinic visit.
- ☐ Review the equipment specialist's report regarding the state of the equipment and any necessary repairs.
    - ☐ Does any of the equipment need to be replaced?
    - ☐ How much will it cost?
- ☐ Are there any maintenance contracts or leases on equipment?

Practice Management Systems

- ☐ What management systems are in place, and are they primarily digital?
    - ☐ If not, estimate the cost of introducing state-of-the-art dental practice software.

Production

- ☐ What percentage is hygiene production of total office production?
    - ☐ How many hygiene days are there per week?
- ☐ How many weeks are the dentist and hygienist booked out by at least seventy percent?
- ☐ How many days does the owner/dentist take off each year?
- ☐ What proportion of endodontics, periodontics, oral surgery, and implant placement is referred out?
- ☐ Obtain up-to-date production records by provider and procedure code.
- ☐ What is the monthly average of short-notice cancellations?
- ☐ How is the acceptance of treatment plans monitored?
- ☐ How many emergency patients are handled per month?

Accounts Receivable

- ☐ Obtain an up-to-date accounts receivable aging report.
    - ☐ What percentage of the accounts receivable are over ninety days?
    - ☐ Will you purchase the accounts receivable?

☐ What percentage of production are collections?

☐ What is the total of credit balances owed to patients?

Future Growth

☐ Analyze the growth trends of the practice.

☐ Does the practice have a marketing or promotional program?

    ☐ How effective is it?

    ☐ Is the website up-to-date?

    ☐ Is the clinic active on social media?

Carrying out a due diligence audit is not for the faint-hearted; it's a lot of work. However, it is vital to your long-term success. While time-consuming, the audit gives you the chance to put the dental practice under the microscope and find out all you need to know about it. In short, it puts you in the driving seat.

The audit may reveal areas that require remedial action or opportunities to boost productivity and reduce expenses. If you hire a dental equipment specialist—as I suggested earlier—their report might list several pieces of equipment in need of urgent repair at an estimated cost of $20,000. If this is the case, you can go back to the seller and give them a choice of making the repairs or taking the amount off the purchase price.

Another common issue is found in a line item in the clinic's accounts receivable. It relates to patient credit balances. These credit balances occur when a patient or insurance company has paid more than they owed. In other words, a credit balance is an amount owed to the patient. These are usually small amounts, but they can add up. For instance, returning to Jordan's purchase, his seller's patient credit balance was $25,000. The question arises as to whether patients will ever receive this money. Jordan's buyer told him that the amounts were very old and small, and his patients were unlikely to request the reimbursement. Jordan wisely sought to have the $25,000 taken off the purchase price. This seemingly minor issue can quickly grow into a serious argument. I've personally seen it jeopardize a million-dollar sale. In the end, the two parties satisfactorily resolved it, but only after many hours of costly negotiations, much of it including lawyers.

Don't be fooled. Do your due diligence and fully understand what you are buying and its actual value. After carrying out your audit you may discover that the practice is not worth the asking price. At that point you can either pull out without any consequences or, perhaps, renegotiate the price or other aspects of the sale.

Do it right the first time, or live to regret it. The last thing you want to do is spend hundreds of thousands of dollars on what an English friend of mine charmingly refers to as a pig in a poke. This excellent idiom dates back to the 1500s when unscrupulous merchants would sell someone a wriggly piglet bound in a burlap sack, sight unseen. When an unwary or easily fooled buyer got the "pig" home, they might discover a couple of rabbits or a chicken in the bag rather than the far more valuable piglet.

Key Takeaways

- [ ] Once the LOI is signed, you take control of the potential transition.

- [ ] Meet the seller and ensure you connect personally and professionally and that your practice philosophies align.

- [ ] Most successful transitions occur when buyer and seller hit it off instantly. If you have trouble bonding with the dentist on your first visit, make it your last.

- [ ] Carrying out a due diligence audit is not for the faint-hearted; it's a lot of work. Fully understand what you are buying and its actual value.

- [ ] Ensure there is a restrictive covenant in any associate's agreement to prevent them from setting up on their own or at another clinic and luring away patients and employees.

- [ ] Identify any deal-breakers and resolve them before carrying out full due diligence.

6

Before You Sign the Purchase Agreement

Okay, you've carried out your due diligence and all looks good; you can now sign the purchase agreement, correct? Not so fast; there's still a ton of stuff in the purchase agreement that can come back to haunt you if you are not careful. You and your lawyer need to analyze the agreement in detail. Talking about lawyers, ensure you retain a lawyer who specializes in dental transitions or who at least has previously dealt with several. You need someone who can help you spot the deal-breakers that may well be hidden in the small print. Remember, you and the seller both want a good deal. The seller is primarily looking for an agreement that minimizes their exposure to post-sale obligations (e.g., patient retreatments or employee severance). Once you sign on the dotted line there is no going back.

Before you begin to review the purchase agreement, consider any unresolved issues emanating from your due diligence, even smaller niggling thoughts or concerns that you might have come across during the process. Make a list of any that you did not fully resolve. Here are a few that I regularly come across.

☐ Confidence in maintaining pre-sale practice revenues.

☐ Long-time lease security (i.e., until you retire).

☐ Your ability to obtain adequate bank financing.

☐ Whether your management style is compatible with the existing practice culture.

Let's look at these four critical issues a little more closely.

Practice Revenues

Cash flow is critical; it's the key thing on which you based your offer. Without it, the whole house of cards could come tumbling down.

- [ ] How confident are you that you can sustain current revenues?

- [ ] On what basis is that confidence founded?

- [ ] What are the fundamental drivers that currently produce sustainable cash flow and bring in new patients?

- [ ] What are the clinic's competitive advantages (e.g., location, favorable demographics, social media exposure, the reputation of the principal dentist)?

- [ ] What effective marketing strategies will you immediately introduce?

- [ ] How can you protect yourself against post-sale events that might jeopardize revenues and the long-term viability of the clinic?

Asking yourself these questions will allow you to identify things you might add to the purchase agreement to help you protect revenues. Your purchase agreement should already include a restrictive covenant on the seller and associates to prevent them from soliciting patients. But will this give you ironclad protection against the loss of patients and employees? You could consider adding a clause to the agreement whereby the seller agrees to promote you as their chosen successor by making personal patient introductions in addition to a "welcome to the new dentist" form letter.

Premises Lease

If you are leasing the premises, is there a potential future tenancy risk? If you took my advice, you probably secured a twenty-year lease option, but what about thirty-plus? For instance, if the premises turn out to be perfect and you plan to practice there for the next twenty years and then sell to a successor, how certain are you that when the time comes you will be able to promise a buyer an ongoing lease?

Fast forward twenty years and consider what a financial blow it would be if you were ready to sell your successful practice and the lease was about to expire with no option to extend. If there was no nearby, suitable location to which you could relocate, your anticipated sales proceeds would shrink to not much more than the value of the patient charts. The most common reason preventing someone from renewing a lease is that there are plans to demolish the building. Before you sign the purchase agreement, speak to the landlord or city planners and get some idea of the probability of the building being demolished in the future. I've known times when this simple exercise has revealed some surprising plans.

Financing the Purchase

Many potential buyers are too casual when approaching lending institutions. Asking for money is a bit of a science, and if you don't want to be disappointed, it's a good idea to have a solid strategy. First, don't sound out an account manager by meeting to casually outline your needs. This approach wastes their time and gets you nowhere. Instead, prepare a formal one-page loan proposal. Presenting a proposal will ensure a good first impression. The proposal should outline how you plan to finance the purchase, your operating capital needs, and the terms you would like from the bank. Accompanying this should be a personal statement of your net worth, along with cash flow projections for both yourself and the dental practice.

The physical act of preparing a loan proposal forces you to consider both your financial needs and your ability to service the loan. In the absence of a specific loan request, bankers are likely to offer you less money than you need and impose unacceptable borrowing conditions. Banks are often willing to finance the purchase of a dental clinic but can be disinclined to provide an adequate operating line of credit. The best advice I can give you is to push hard for the amount you need during the first negotiations with the bank. You must ensure you have the working capital you need for marketing and other essential expenditures, not to mention those that come out of left field. It will be significantly more challenging to go back to the trough for more later. Bankers hate when you go back for seconds.

If you are uncomfortable negotiating with the bank, retain a professional to handle the financial institution. Most dentists I deal with detest the thought of hard bargaining with a loan manager. If you would rather dance with a gorilla than negotiate with your banker, get your advisor to do it. Many CPAs or transition consultants have successively handled bank negotiations and do not fear bargaining hard for their clients.

Financial institutions are often reluctant to immediately finance both a practice purchase and the clinic real estate. It does, however, depend on your financial situation. Although they prefer to lend money to purchase hard assets, they will still want to see you sustain a history of solid cash flow before they become amenable to supporting you in buying the property. In light of this, you may want to negotiate with the seller to purchase the real estate at a later date. For a firm timeline, ask your banker.

Now is the time to review the clinic's operating cash flow and determine how it will be affected by your expected debt servicing costs. To do this, use the break-even formula I outlined in chapter three. It will immediately show how close you are to breaking even (i.e., revenues equal expenses resulting in zero income). Think of the break-even point like a gas gauge; it tells you when you have run out of fuel.

Knowing the Workplace Culture

It is unlikely that when you carried out the due diligence you had much, if any, contact with the clinic staff. Most buyers are keen to keep the sale a secret, particularly in the early stages of negotiation. It's probably due to this fact that I have never seen "workplace culture" on a due diligence checklist.

You must get an idea of the workplace culture before signing the purchase contract. Positive workplace culture is crucial in driving practice success. It attracts high-quality staff, fosters contentment, and creates job satisfaction. In a positive environment you will experience minimal staff turnover and quickly fill any vacancies. When employees are appreciated, everyday job performance is high, and patients become fans of the clinic and help bring in new business.

You may be thinking that it is what it is, and it's something you can figure out later. If it's good, excellent; if it's terrible, you'll fix it. Once again, if only it were that simple. Until you become familiar with the existing practice culture, you have no idea whether your practice philosophy and management style will meld with the current office culture. The consequences of misaligned workplace cultures can be devastating.

One of my clients, Sandra, sold her practice two years ago to a guy I'll call Allen. Sandra was a good dentist and a good boss. For twenty five years the clinic had run smoothly, and everyone got along. Someone once referred to Sandra as a cheerleader rather than a traditional boss. She noticed employees' achievements, offered encouragement, and empowered her staff to make decisions. Patients loved that there was always a pleasant welcome and atmosphere. The clinic was always getting referrals from delighted patients. Staff turnover was low, and when someone did leave, there was a healthy number of qualified applicants—many referred by her employees.

Then Allen took over and everything went awry. As good a boss as Sandra was, she never thought to introduce Allen during the final negotiation stages of the sale, and Allen had never asked to meet the staff. Like many new owners, he was parachuted in on a Monday morning and introduced to the team as the new owner—and their new boss. There was shock, horror, and an apocalyptic effect on the employees. Allen wasn't warm and fuzzy like Sandra, so the resentment was almost immediate. He came across like a cost accountant. Allen's number one priority was to recoup his $1 million investment as soon as possible, and he saw employees as an overhead item. He never recognized the incredible office culture that was the foundation of the dental practice. More importantly, he did not recognize its immense value.

Allen failed to understand that he had paid Sandra for the clinic's goodwill, goodwill that was "owned" and "controlled" by the staff. He never realized that if the clinic experience stays the same after a sale, 95% of patients will remain loyal.

Instead, he immediately introduced cost-cutting measures, which quickly led to shortages in basic dental supplies. It took only three months for Allen to kill an office culture that had taken more than twenty years to establish. Almost all staff left, and patients eagerly followed them to other clinics. Allen tried to rebuild the clinic, but the dental community was small, and the word was out; he struggled to find good, experienced staff and enough new patients to replace those he had lost. It wasn't long before he bailed and sold what was left of the practice, suffering a huge loss.

The moral of this story is that you need to ask yourself whether your practice philosophy and management style fits with the office culture of the seller. And you won't know that unless you meet the staff and spend a little time in the clinic. As I mentioned earlier, the challenge is that sellers don't want you to meet their employees before the sale because they want to keep the practice transition a secret.

You may feel that you will manage the corporate culture issue without meeting the staff. Maybe you can, but it is a risk. Only you can decide whether it is a risk worth taking. My advice is to insist on meeting the staff before you sign that purchase agreement.

The Purchase Agreement Dissected

The following crib sheet is offered as a guide to the considerations you should make when reviewing a purchase agreement. It should not replace the advice and guidance of your professional transition team.

1. Assets included in the sale:

    a. Practice goodwill. To include:

        i. a comprehensive patient database containing contact information, patient records, charts, X-rays and models, and all relevant treatment documentation.

        ii. existing telephone number(s)

        iii. email addresses

        iv. website(s)

        v. trade name(s)

        vi. social media accounts

        vii. any information relevant to running the practice

    b. All leasehold property and improvements.

    c. All office furniture, equipment, computer hardware and software, hand instruments, surgical instruments, and other chattels used in running the practice.

    d. All inventory and supplies used in connection with the operation of the practice.

2. Assets excluded from the sale:

    a. Cash on hand or on deposit at the Closing Date.

    b. All artwork, textbooks, and personal mementos of the seller.

    c. All accounts receivable of the practice as at the Closing Date.

3. Seller's liabilities:

    a. All accounts payable of the practice due and owing as of the Closing Date.

    b. All liabilities, lease obligations, and shareholder loans.

4. Purchase price allocation:

    In an asset sale, sales proceeds must be allocated to the various asset types, such as equipment, leaseholds, supplies, patient charts, etc. For tax purposes, this allocation is based on the fair market value of the assets.

    Allocation of asset types can often be a contentious point for buyers and sellers, and can result in significant haggling. The difficulty arises because the two parties are on opposite sides of tax law. You, the buyer, will want to maximize your tax write-offs by expensing or depreciating the tangible assets rather than the goodwill, which is amortized over many years. On the other hand, the seller wants the reverse of this so that they can reduce income taxes by favoring an allocation of the proceeds to the goodwill rather than to the depreciable assets.

    It's a zero-sum game. The extra tax amount saved by you becomes an additional tax cost for the seller. I suggest you leave the bargaining over the purchase price allocation to your dental CPA, who has likely handled many similar situations.

    The asset allocation, as described above, is only necessary during an asset sale. If the dental practice corporation's stock is sold, there is no need to allocate assets.

5. Retreatment:

    You will need to agree on whose responsibility it is to carry out retreatments on patients post-sale. Hopefully, by the time you get to this discussion you will have gotten to know the dentist and carried out your due diligence. You will understand the seller's reputation as a dentist and will have some idea of the level of risk you face from their patients returning for retreatment. However, you'll have little idea of the scope of retreatments that might be necessary.

    If the seller does not continue as an associate in the practice, the purchase and sale agreement should clearly state the course of action when a patient comes back to have work redone.

    The choices are simple; if a patient requires additional treatment, you can either perform the rework yourself and charge the seller or have the seller complete the work free of charge.

    Unfortunately, things are rarely that straightforward. Sellers are often concerned about the possibility of the buyer charging them for unnecessary treatments that could cost them a lot of money.

Here are the options/clauses your lawyer might use in the purchase agreement. Appropriate monetary amounts and time limitations can be attached, and your lawyer can turn them into legalese. These will safeguard you and formalize any course of action.

- Should the buyer believe it necessary to redo dental work at no charge to the patient, they will notify the seller. The seller will then be obliged to re-treat the patient and is responsible for associated lab fees.

- Should the buyer consider it necessary to redo dental work but fails to notify the seller, the seller will not reimburse the buyer. If the buyer notifies the seller and requests that the buyer handles the retreatment, the seller will refund the buyer for the cost of the treatment.

- The seller's responsibility for retreatment will be for an agreed period (usually between twelve and twenty-four months from the closing date).

Note: As there is much uncertainty about the scope of possible retreatment, a good strategy might be to suggest that the seller reduce their selling price in return for removing the retreatment clause. In my experience, an amount between $10,000 to $20,000 is reasonable. Remember, if the seller agrees to this, you will have no further recourse against the seller for any retreatments.

6. The seller's accounts receivable:

If you decide not to purchase the accounts receivable, you need to establish a system that allows you to collect the receivables on behalf of the seller. You should avoid having the seller collect the outstanding receivables directly; remember, this is now your business. In either case, you should take into consideration patient goodwill.

The agreement should stipulate how many months the buyer will collect the seller's accounts receivable. If you collect them on behalf of the seller, then a collection fee of between five percent and ten percent is appropriate.

7. Restrictive covenants:

You must protect the clinic's income stream by including in the purchase agreement a covenant that prevents the seller from competing with your clinic after the sale. Bear in mind that the seller's legal adviser will carefully review the enforceability of any restrictive covenant. To be enforceable, the restrictions put on the seller must be reasonable both in terms of length and geographical scope. Even if the seller does not own another practice, the seller should be restricted from providing dental services through any type of arrangement, for example, as an associate, partner, consultant, or shareholder.

If the seller remains an associate, it is common to have the restrictive covenant start from the last day the associate works in the clinic, not from the day the practice is sold.

8. Non-solicitation of patients and employees:

It is common to include a covenant preventing the seller from soliciting patients for five to ten years after the sale. If the seller breaches this covenant, the buyer can require the seller to pay damages based on the revenues billed to the patients.

Similarly, many sales agreements prohibit the seller from soliciting employees, usually for a period of five years. If a seller breaches this agreement, you can sue for damages. Damages can amount to $20,000 per employee.

9. Assignment of lease:

You should ensure that all tenant's rights under the lease are transferred to you as an agreement of the sale. This crucial step will give you a direct tenant relationship with the landlord. Most leases require the landlord's consent for such an assignment.

Take into consideration that you may be required to assure your lender that the lease covers the loan term. For example, if your loan amortization is ten years, lenders will want to know that the clinic can operate out of that space for the entire ten-year period.

10. Vendor's representations and warranties:

Representations and warranties are the most critical part of the agreement. Here are some of the representations and warranties you will require from the seller:

1. The title to all practice assets is free and clear of any liens, claims, or other encumbrances.

2. Proof that the seller's license to practice dentistry has never been suspended or revoked.

3. The seller knows of no pending court actions, lawsuits, or claims.

4. The practice income and expenses are materially correct.

5. The seller has not engaged in any practice billing procedures that might violate the terms of any third-party insurance contract.

6. The seller is unaware of anything that exists or is likely to arise that would adversely affect the practice's operation after the sale.

In return, the seller will usually ask you to acknowledge that any income and expense projections provided to you are projections only and are not a representation or warranty relating to the future income and expenses of the practice.

You, of course, may want to insist that the seller provides a warranty for any financial projections. This assurance would allow you to, potentially, take legal action against the seller for misrepresentation if the actual results fell short of their income projections.

11. Assisting with the transition:

It is impossible to force a seller to promote the practice once it is under new ownership. But at a minimum, you should expect some cooperative provisions in the agreement. These might include the seller agreeing to:

a) Sign and distribute a letter of introduction to all patients.

b) Act in good faith when transferring the practice's goodwill to the buyer.

c) Consult with, and advise, the buyer for six to nine months after the sale, at no cost.

Key Takeaways

☐ Deal with any unresolved issues from your due diligence, even smaller niggling thoughts or concerns.

☐ Protect practice revenues in the purchase agreement.

☐ Fully understand and assess potential future tenancy risks.

☐ Develop a strategy for approaching lending institutions. Be professional. Retain the services of a professional transition specialist if you are uncomfortable dealing with banks.

☐ Once you have the figures, review the clinic's operating cash flow and determine how it will be affected by your expected debt servicing costs.

☐ You must get an idea of the workplace culture before signing the purchase contract. Positive workplace culture is crucial in driving practice success.

☐ Dissect and analyze the purchase agreement. Once you sign on the dotted line, there is no going back.

7

Purchasing a Partial Interest

I am often asked about options that don't involve taking a giant leap into full ownership and assuming the responsibility of running an existing dental practice. One way is to start your own dental practice from scratch, but that's a whole other story—I suggest you read my upcoming book on starting your own practice, or call me at Purtzki Transitions for advice.

The other option is to investigate a co-ownership arrangement. It's not uncommon for dentists to work in group practices; in fact, many prefer this model. If you come across such an opportunity, it will typically involve a mid-career dentist working to maximum capacity who has reached a plateau in terms of production. The two most common arrangements, which I will discuss in this chapter, are *solo group* and *partnership.*

Usually, a transition to retirement is not the selling dentist's desired objective. They may want to reduce the amount of time they work in the practice, or they wish to pursue a specialty and need someone to assume the clinic's general dentistry commitments. Alternatively, they may be looking to grow the practice and can see an opportunity to bring in more patients. This could result from a fast-growing community, or perhaps a competing clinic has closed or relocated.

Solo Group Practice

In this scenario you would first join another dentist's practice as an associate. Being an associate is vital, as only after gaining first-hand experience working with the clinic's patients, staff, and your new colleagues can you decide whether or not you would like to spend your dental career at the practice. Being involved in the clinic's daily operations allows you to establish its profitability and confidently project the practice cash flow you might expect to receive as an owner.

In practical terms, you enter into an agreement whereby you purchase an interest in the practice once you become established (i.e., reach pre-agreed revenue targets and develop a patient base). This usually takes about two years. Achieving these targets assures your prospective partner that you will be able to meet your financial obligations regarding practice overhead and at the same time cover your living expenses.

The senior dentist will likely build into your agreement a three to six month trial period, during which either party can walk away. During this period, they will monitor your relationship with staff, your professionalism, leadership skills, energy, commitment, the way you deal with patients, and of course, the quality of your dentistry.

You will be required to make a good-faith deposit, usually after a short trial period. Once the trial period is over and you both agree to move forward, you will be expected to make a sizable, refundable deposit. If finance is a challenge for you, the deposit can sometimes take the form of sweat equity. For instance, an agreed amount could be withheld from your monthly remuneration and held in trust by the practice.

Some dentists may attempt to value the practice after you have reached the pre-set revenue targets. This is a disincentive to building your practice, as the better you do, the more you will have to pay to become a partner. Instead, insist on valuing the practice at the beginning of the relationship or associateship. For this example, let's assume the total practice value is $800,000, with $600,000 attributable to goodwill and $200,000 for tangible assets, equipment, etc. Two years later, at the time of your purchase, a new valuation is carried out, and the practice value has increased by $400,000 to $1.2 million. This increase is all attributable to an increase in goodwill that is the result of increased patient flow (much of which you brought in).

For argument's sake, let's assume both you and your prospective partner treated approximately the same number of new patients over that period. If we take the new valuation, you—if you are buying half of the practice— would be on the hook for $600,000. However, in my experience, it is reasonable for you to suggest you receive a fifty percent discount on the $400,000 increase to the value of the practice. In our example above, this would result in a purchase price of $500,000. This takes into account the fact that you were responsible for half of the increase in the value of the practice.

A *solo group* partnership may suit you if you want to be your own boss with your own practice but enjoy the benefit of sharing operating costs with an established dentist.

The Cost-Sharing Arrangement

After the purchase, you will no longer receive a percentage of your production; you will be in a cost-sharing arrangement where you receive all your production, and perhaps a share of hygiene revenue. You will then be required to contribute to the practice overhead based on an agreed cost-sharing formula.

It is crucial to have a written agreement with your new partner that outlines all the elements involved in cost-sharing. This agreement underscores the importance of the arrangement and will also reduce misunderstandings. The agreement should be developed by a lawyer and tailored to meet the specific needs of both you and the dentist with whom you will be partnering.

Here are some examples of the essential provisions that you will need to include. But remember, these are only examples to provide you with a starting point.

Hygiene Revenues

Each dentist will be entitled to hygiene revenue from patients assigned to their respective practice. In turn, they will be responsible for the salary and benefits of the clinic's hygienists on a pro-rata basis. For example, if one dentist receives sixty percent of hygiene revenues, they will pay sixty percent of hygienists' salaries and benefits.

New Dentists

Neither party will engage or hire an associate for three (3) years after the partnership's commencement date unless each dentist's practice has at least one thousand (1,000) active patients or unless otherwise mutually agreed. An *active patient* is deemed to be a patient who has visited the hygiene department at the clinic at least once in the prior two (2) years.

Should the dentists jointly decide to engage an associate or specialist, the terms of engagement will be determined mutually. All net revenues from the shared associate or specialist's services will be shared equally by the dentists.

If either dentist individually hires or engages an associate or specialist, all revenue and expenses related to that hire are the responsibility of that partner.

Either partner shall be entitled to retain a locum as reasonably required without the written consent of the other dentist.

Associate Revenues

If the dentists decide to bring on board an additional associate, the partners will determine the terms of engagement. The associates' net revenue contribution to the practice will be divided equally by the dentists unless otherwise mutually agreed.

Shared Expenses

Each party shall contribute equally to the shared expenses, except for dental supplies, which will be charged as a percentage of each dentist's production.

Capital Expenditures

Any capital expenditures related to the practice will require joint approval. All approved capital expenditures will be shared equally. The dentists agree to prepare an annual budget for this purpose. All capital expenditures which relate solely to an individual dentist's practice will be borne exclusively by that individual.

Bank and Internal Accounting Arrangements

The parties will open and maintain a joint bank account from which shared expenses will be paid. The partners will review the account monthly to ensure there are sufficient funds to meet the practice's financial obligations.

Practice Hours

The partners will jointly agree the dates and times for each dentist to practice dentistry at the premises. Each dentist agrees to limit their respective practice of dentistry to the dates and times outlined in the calendar, except with the consent of the other dentist.

Patient Allocation

Unless otherwise mutually agreed, new patients will be allocated on an equal basis (using best efforts). Where patients request the services of a specific dentist, they will be referred to that dentist. Patients who do not specify a preference will be allocated in such a way as to equalize the total number of new patients referred to each dentist.

Short-Term Disability

Should either dentist become disabled for a period not exceeding six weeks, the other dentist will provide clinical care to the disabled dentist's patients for up to ten hours per week at no cost to the disabled dentist and perform all necessary hygiene checks.

This agreement will ensure coverage for that portion of the disabled dentist's overhead expenses, which are not covered by short-term disability insurance, and help maintain hygiene production. Each dentist will need to consult their respective insurance broker to ensure that this arrangement does not conflict with the terms of the dentists' short-term disability insurance policies.

The Buy-Sell Agreement

The buy-sell agreement deals with retirement, disability, death, and malpractice in a group practice and provides for an orderly exit. This agreement is crucial, its provisions will preserve both partners' equity in the practice. Never use a boilerplate document that offers standardized solutions. Work with a lawyer to draw up a document that reflects the specific needs of you and your partner.

The following will give you an idea of the key elements that make up a buy-sell agreement.

Restrictions on Transfer

No dentist shall sell or transfer their interest in the practice unless specific provisions are met as outlined below.

Sales to Third Party

Neither partner is permitted to sell their interest to a third party unless that person has agreed to abide by the existing cost-sharing and buy-sell agreements already in place.

Right of First Refusal to Purchase

A standard clause in these agreements is the right of first refusal. It states that no dentist shall sell or transfer their practice to another dentist unless they have first offered it to their partner.

There are two basic types of right of first refusal.

1. The selling partner obtains a third-party offer that is either cash or unconditional. In this case, the seller gives notice to the remaining dentist and provides them with details of the offer. The remaining dentist has first right of refusal to match the offer on the same terms and conditions. If they refuse, the seller can sell the practice to a third party.

    This scenario is not ideal for the selling dentist because potential buyers may be reticent to invest time and money in preparing an unconditional offer when the remaining dentist gets right of first refusal. However, the remaining dentist is in a better position as they can review the third-party offer and decide whether they are prepared to work with the new dentist. Or, if they choose to buy out their partner, all the work in preparing the offer has been done for them.

2. In the second scenario, the selling dentist tells their partner that they would like to sell their practice and submits their terms and conditions. The remaining dentist then has an opportunity to either accept or reject the offer. If they reject the offer, the seller can sell their interest to a third party within a prescribed period. However, the terms and conditions of a third-party sale cannot be more favorable than those offered to the remaining dentist.

    This scenario favors the seller because they don't need to find a purchaser first. On the other hand, the remaining dentist has no guarantee as to whom their partner might sell their practice to if they turn the offer down. This uncertainty puts them in a difficult position, and they may feel pressure to submit an offer to purchase.

Restrictive Covenant

In the case of any sale, the seller will be required to agree to the usual restrictive covenants regarding practicing within a specific geographic radius and the solicitation of patients and employees.

Mandatory Withdrawal

If one partner receives a license suspension or acts in a manner that results in the practice suffering an unacceptable hit to its reputation in the dental community, the departing dentist will be required to sell the practice to the other dentist. The purchase price will be discounted by fifty percent, based on a fair-market valuation, and must be paid within 60 days.

Buy/Sell on Death

In the case of the death of a cost-share partner, the purchase price of the practice must be paid in full by the remaining dentist. A compulsory buy-out upon death clause is crucial to avoid the deceased's estate being burdened with a dental clinic that has no marketable value.

If a surviving partner can't afford the buy-out it can cause multiple problems, including patient attrition, which can be extensive and rapid when a dentist dies. To avoid this situation, the buy-sell agreement should include a funding mechanism to provide cash in the case of the death of a partner. One way to achieve this is to purchase life insurance on each dentist with the other partner named as the beneficiary. The amount of life insurance purchased can be agreed upon by the partners in advance as a reasonable buy-out price in the case of death, or it can be determined by carrying out a practice valuation.

If the partners choose not to purchase life insurance, an alternative could be an agreement to gradually pay out the value of the deceased dentist's interest in the clinic to their estate, in monthly installments, for a year starting from the date of death.

Buy/Sell and Long-Term Disability

If a dentist becomes disabled for more than a year, the remaining dentist is required to purchase the disabled dentist's practice at a ten percent discount based on practice valuation, to be paid in monthly installments over an agreed period (usually six- to twelve-months). The parties may arrange for a disability buy-out insurance policy. However, most practitioners don't do this because these insurance policies can be prohibitively expensive.

Mandatory Retirement

The most likely reason a senior dentist withdraws from their practice is to retire, so I am always amazed that buy-sell agreements rarely address the looming issue of retirement. I always advise clients to add a withdrawal clause guaranteeing a retirement buy-out if a successor can't be found.

Termination Clause

The agreement shall terminate:

- ☐ If either party goes into bankruptcy or proposes to its creditors.

- ☐ If either party dies, or they become disabled for more than one year.

- ☐ If the parties agree in writing to the termination of the agreement.

Partnership

A partnership arrangement starts the same way as the *solo group* option. The seller is likely a busy dentist with a growing practice who, for one of the reasons mentioned at the beginning of this chapter, is looking for a partner. It could also be that they are looking to spend more time with their family and to cash in a portion of the equity they have invested in the practice.

Most partnerships are corporate entities. Instead of buying one-half of the practice's assets as in the *solo group* model, under the partnership model you may be required to purchase the stock of the selling corporation to become a 50/50 partner. I suggest you talk with your CPA about the significant tax differences between buying assets and stock and allow them to advise you on what is more beneficial in your situation.

It's possible that after discussing options with a prospective partner, you may decide to have two separate corporations. With this arrangement, a management company is usually set up to manage the clinic, track the revenues, and pay expenses.

There are pros and cons to a partnership. Dentists are raised on the *eat-what-you-kill* model and don't like to share their revenues. Often the direct operating expenses, including dental supplies, are also based on the partner's production. However, the essence of a partnership is the sharing of profits regardless of who generates the income. Also, as a partner, you have to fulfill your obligations to the partnership. You are obliged to take joint responsibility for the practice management, which may include committing to a minimum of hours of working in the clinic and potentially incurring financial penalties if you decide to quit the partnership.

On the positive side, a partnership makes it easier to add new partners by selling a share of the partnership. This type of agreement is becoming more popular because it allows dentists to share the management burden and achieve a better work-life balance.

Key Takeaways

☐ The two most common co-ownership arrangements are *solo group* and *partnership*.

☐ In *solo group*, you first join another dentist's practice as an associate. An associateship gives you valuable first-hand clinic experience before you decide to become a partner.

☐ Value the practice at the beginning of the relationship or associateship rather than after you have reached pre-set revenue targets.

☐ A *solo group* partnership may suit you if you want to be your own boss with your own practice but enjoy the benefit of sharing operating costs with an established dentist.

☐ A *partnership* arrangement starts the same way as the *solo group* option. However, instead of buying one-half of the practice's assets as in the *solo group* model, you may be required to purchase the stock of the selling corporation to become a 50/50 partner.

☐ Partnership agreements are becoming more popular because they allow dentists to share the management burden and achieve a better work-life balance.

8

Your First 30 Days of Practice Ownership

Let's jump forward. You took all my advice and purchased a great dental practice. After being an associate for several years, you are looking forward to being the master of your own destiny. Unfortunately, I have witnessed many dentists in your position fail to take full responsibility for the practice they now own. Many new owners carry on as if they are still associates. They enjoy dentistry and treating patients every day but avoid taking responsibility for managing the practice. In effect, they leave the clinic to run on autopilot. I cannot urge you enough to step into, and embrace, the leadership role that is crucial to your clinic's success. You don't want the practice that you got a great deal on become a money pit.

The first 30 days after becoming a practice owner are crucial to the future success of your clinic. Working *on* your practice as well as *in* it is essential. You have a short window to put your stamp on the practice and make any changes that you feel are necessary. "A new broom sweeps clean" in this situation. If you want to adopt a new business approach, you must immediately implement your new plan. Hopefully, you will have developed a new, well-thought-out business plan which you can share with your office manager if you have one. You must demonstrate that you have carefully considered the future and that you are not planning to run the clinic by the seat of your pants. Do it right and you will be rewarded with significant practice growth, giving you more income, a happier staff, and satisfied patients. If you miss the opportunity, you will be forever stuck following in the footsteps of the previous owner.

Your employees will expect you to take control and be their new leader, but don't be a dictator. Sit down with them individually and encourage them to tell you what works in the clinic and what doesn't. This strategy will pay dividends later. Getting to know their strengths and insights into how the clinic operates will be invaluable and help you gain their respect. Consider this as your first team-building exercise.

If you carried out sufficient due diligence before purchasing the practice, you should have already analyzed the current staffing requirements and associated wage costs. Hopefully, you will have also done a break-even analysis (as outlined in Chapter 3). It will project the clinic's operating costs in relation to estimated revenues and cash flow. This analysis will also determine the minimum revenues you require to cover your operating expenses, including debt servicing before you receive any compensation. The point of zero income and zero loss is the break-even point.

In those precious first thirty days you should prepare revenue and staff cost projections and formulate a realistic cash flow spreadsheet for your first twenty-four months. I cannot over-emphasize how invaluable these forecasts are; they provide a benchmark for comparing your projections to actual results. Treat them as an early warning device that allows you to take remedial action quickly, should the clinic not perform as well as you had hoped in the early days of the new ownership transition.

Controlling Your Overhead

The new practice owner's biggest headache is controlling overhead. This is especially true for new owners who must pay off the practice loan and need enough to cover personal and living expenses. The need for sufficient cash flow is urgent and imperative; it's crucial to know your practice's overhead. Don't make the mistake of believing you will find this figure in the income statement prepared by the practice's accountant, as it's unlikely to be there. Accountants prepare reports for tax purposes rather than for you to use as a management tool.

To calculate your practice's overhead, calculate the collectible practice revenues after making all fee adjustments. Then, tally all expenses directly related to the practice's operation, including lab fees, dental supplies, staff salaries, facility costs, office expenses, marketing costs, clinic insurance, bank charges, and accounting fees.

Exclude financial costs (e.g., bank loan interest and lease payments) discretionary expenses (e.g., continuing education, salaries to "non-working" family members, auto expenses, and travel). Also, exclude non-cash items such as depreciation and amortization; they are purely accounting calculations. Once you have a final figure for your expenses, divide it by the figure you reached for your practice revenues. This calculation will show you what percentage of your revenue is taken by overhead. For instance, if your practice revenue is $900,000 and your expenses are $567,000, the overhead is 63% ($567,000/$900,000).

As a new owner, you will naturally want to reduce overhead. The big question is, is that the best or wisest thing to do? Unless you have bought a massively overstaffed clinic, it isn't easy to trim expenses without damaging growth. For instance, if you manage to cut dental supply costs by 30% (from 10% of gross to 7%), the harsh reality is that you have only managed to reduce your overhead by 3%.

A better way to become more profitable is to increase revenues. Let me explain; if you increase your clinic's gross revenues from $800,000 to $1 million, your 70% overhead will drop to 60%. You will increase your net income by 60%, from $240,000 to $400,000. Please note I have assumed that all costs remain the same except for variable expenses (i.e., dental supplies and lab costs at 20% of gross revenues).

You may be thinking it's easy for Manfred to tell me to increase revenues, but that's not easy in a competitive environment. Sure, it's always tough building a dental practice, but the reality is that many clinics sit back and wait for patients to walk through the door. In my experience, those that are proactive in marketing and selling their services meet a receptive audience. Many dentists advertise their clinics; few actively sell to prospective new patients. There is a big difference. If you want to bring in new patients, you need a skilled receptionist trained to convert inquiries into a practice visit. Every employee has to realize that they are part of the sales team. Getting a person from phone inquiry to an in-person visit to a long-term patient requires everyone at the clinic to be welcoming, kind, efficient, and professional.

The Office Manager: A Lynchpin

In the last few pages, I have probably scared you silly with the amount of "management stuff" for which you need to be responsible. The journey from associate to owner is not without its bumps and bruises. Assuming that your staff members are fully occupied doing their jobs, I strongly recommend investing in a full-time office manager. If you want to grow your practice beyond your expectations, you need someone who can stickhandle the day-to-day management of the practice and help you turn your business plan and financial projections into reality.

Finding a good office manager is easier than you might think. There are many good, underutilized office managers at other clinics who are bored by routine work and a lack of challenge. As a new owner with new plans, you can offer them an exciting and challenging career opportunity.

Once you have a new office manager, they should implement your business plan. First, they should streamline the clinic's accounting system to produce weekly and monthly practice monitors and income statements. Once they have achieved this critical task, they should improve the management information system, update social media sites, and ensure the clinic's website is current and glitch-free.

If the clinic doesn't already have one, your office manager should develop a policy and procedures manual that includes job-specific expectations, performance-based staff evaluations, and salary reviews. HR is an integral part of an office manager's job, so they need to be an effective people-problem solver. Internal conflict is insidious in a dental practice; it permeates the atmosphere quickly. Patients become exposed to the toxicity, feel uncomfortable, and promptly leave to find a new clinic.

As I said earlier, there are many good office managers. However, very few are given any formal training in practice management. My advice is to find an experienced person and provide them with opportunities for personal development. Do it right, and you will own a clinic that runs like a well-oiled machine with motivated staff and up-to-date management accounts.

Creating a Championship Team

It's easy to consider your patients as the most important people to your practice, but in reality your employees are far more critical. What would be more devastating? Having your favorite patient leave and go to another dentist, or seeing your skilled, energetic, and hardworking hygienist go to work for the dentist next door? The financial impact of losing a patient to another clinic is minimal compared to significant hygiene downtime.

There's no shortage of jobs in dentistry. You need your team more than they need you, so treat them well. I worked with a clinic some time ago where their much loved and super-efficient front desk person left unexpectedly. Production dropped precipitously when the practice was unable to fill the position quickly.

Hiring Staff

Hiring good employees is critical; take it seriously by establishing specific hiring criteria for each position. It is easy to fall into the trap of hiring a candidate because they look good on paper and interview well but are unsuited to the job. If you find yourself struggling to find the ideal combination of positive attitude and excellent skills, hire for attitude and train for skill. Beware candidates who exhibit excellent skills but have a negative attitude. Talented people with poor attitudes will lower morale, make your life miserable, and ask for a hefty severance when you inevitably terminate their employment. Look for people whose character and values match those of your practice.

As the most critical aspect of running your practice, give hiring the importance it deserves. Finally, never delegate hiring; by all means involve your office manager, but be the final judge when it comes to all hiring decisions.

Managing Staff

Once you have a great team, you must keep that team together as a cohesive unit. Here are a few tips on building solid relationships with employees.

1. Maintain the same professional relationship with your employees that you have with your patients. Be objective and fair. Don't become too familiar with any one member of staff. Playing favorites creates a toxic environment. Fraternization, however innocent, can later turn the boss's pet into an incoming lawsuit, with the person citing wrongful dismissal or worse.

2. You can be professional and still be happy, friendly, and enthusiastic. Enthusiasm is the fuel that will drive your practice forward. Celebrate the good days and the excellent work of your employees. Constantly looking for and recognizing positive behaviors builds enthusiasm.

3. Create an environment where staff can have a positive work-life balance. Employees look for a harmonious balance between their

career and personal life. Give it to them, and you will see production increase. Ask yourself, how can I manage things so that my employees get what they need while at the same time we achieve our business goals? There is always a win-win if you look hard enough.

4. Be a team builder. Create an organizational culture where employees are part of the decision-making process. For instance, involve staff when hiring new people, renovating the office, or purchasing new equipment. Instill a belief that the team can achieve more working together than working individually, while at the same time valuing each person's unique contribution.

5. Allow people to fail. Encourage your employees to take on new responsibilities without the fear of failure. People learn new skills and grow as much by getting things wrong as they do by getting them right.

6. Be honest with your feedback and give constructive criticism. Your employees are adults; they can handle the truth about what they are doing right and what they need to improve. Feedback must be immediate, given respectfully, and not wait for the annual performance review.

7. Empower your staff to handle situations with patients, suppliers, and coworkers by providing them with guidelines and parameters, so they feel safe to make decisions. An office culture of empowerment is firmly rooted in the foundation of mutual respect and trust. Work environments that empower staff attract the best employees.

Out of the Box Thinking

One of my clients, Sam, treats his staff well and takes it to the next level. The following story is legendary. Out of the blue one day, Sam called a staff meeting for 2 pm on a regular workday. His staff was anxious. This was not normal. A few days earlier, Amy, who works at the front desk, was told to change patient appointments to accommodate Sam's instruction that every employee was to attend the meeting, even those on their day off.

The buzz around the office was that they would probably be reviewing office procedures and production statistics; maybe there would be a strategic planning session. Business was good, so no one thought anything sinister was about to happen, but everyone was nervous. Sam asked everyone to leave the building at the appointed hour, and he locked up. He led them to the street where several limousines waited. The limos took them all to a jewelry store where they could choose a piece of jewelry from a beautiful selection. Afterward, the limos took them to a nearby luxury spa. The employees spent an afternoon enjoying massages, facials, and total relaxation. I often visit Sam at his office, and I have never witnessed employees so pumped, excited, and committed. The atmosphere in his clinic is electric, and whenever he needs to hire new people, his inbox overflows with applications from the very best in the business.

Do the unexpected. Be generous. There is no quicker way to turn your employees into fans. Sam's staff may forget about the bonus they received last year, but they will never forget the surprise trip to the spa.

You don't need to be as creative as Sam, although I would applaud you if you were. But consider, in addition to the obligatory Christmas party, hosting a summer barbeque and allowing staff to bring family members and their children. It is a great way to build camaraderie. Or, perhaps arrange for a tray of baked goods from different bakeries once a week. On a dreary afternoon in the dead of winter, put a large box of high-end chocolates in the staff room with a thank you note to lift spirits and overall morale. A practice with rigid work rules and a humorless dentist who believes in the all-work-no-play philosophy will become morgue-like, and not like Sam's thriving practice where his employees look forward to coming to work every day.

Key Takeaways

- ☐ It is vital that once you become an owner or partner, you accept the responsibilities of management. Don't fall into the trap of remaining an "associate."

- ☐ The first thirty days after becoming a practice owner are crucial to the future success of your clinic. Working *on* your practice as well as *in* it will be essential. You have a short window to put your stamp on the practice and make any changes that you feel are necessary.

- ☐ A well-thought-out business plan is essential, and you need to share it with the office manager.

- ☐ Don't underestimate the value of a good office manager. If you are not inheriting one, consider hiring one.

- ☐ Take control and be a leader (not a dictator). Meet with all staff individually and learn what works and doesn't work in the clinic.

☐ Prepare revenue and staff cost projections and formulate a realistic cash flow spreadsheet for your first twenty-four months.

☐ Focus on revenues by focusing on selling as well as marketing. Every staff member is part of the sales team.

☐ Hire for attitude, train for skill.

☐ Treat your employees like rock stars.

9

The Road to Financial Success

If you follow the guidelines in this book, you will very likely make a sound investment decision on buying a dental practice. But, from the second you take over responsibility for the clinic, every action you take will either make the practice more or less profitable and successful. The transition to new ownership will affect the business no matter how sympathetic you are to how the previous owner ran the clinic.

As I mentioned earlier in this book, do not make the mistake of carrying on as if you are an associate and letting the practice run on autopilot. The decisions you make during the early days of building your practice as an owner will determine whether you are financially successful. Start as you mean to go on—in control.

Focusing on Growth—First Steps

As soon as you get the keys to the clinic, hit the ground running by asking yourself and your office manager or critical staff members these growth-related questions.

- [ ] How can we improve our ability to communicate with our patients?
- [ ] Can we fine-tune how we present treatment plans to patients?
- [ ] How can we ensure wait times for an appointment are no greater than two weeks?

☐ Should we explore opening the clinic for non-traditional hours, including evenings and weekends?

☐ Does the clinic's management system produce financial reports shortly after every month-end?

☐ Are our business systems state-of-the-art?

☐ Which parameters will help us monitor growth and ensure practice profitability? For example:

    ☐ Annual production per patient

    ☐ New patient conversion

    ☐ Treatment acceptance

    ☐ Hygiene revenue as a percentage of total revenues

    ☐ Yearly production per full-time employee

    ☐ Accounts receivables over 60-days

    ☐ Reactivation rate of inactive patients

☐ Can we improve our website and social media presence?

☐ Should we consider other means of marketing?

☐ Are there opportunities for community involvement, such as sponsoring free mouthguards to youth sports teams?

☐ What is our projected net operating income for the next couple of years?

☐ Over the next twenty-four months, what are our monthly projections for the following?

    ☐ New hygiene patients

    ☐ Hygiene patients who require further treatment

    ☐ Estimated revenues for hygiene patients and recall frequency

    ☐ New patients requiring treatment

    ☐ New emergency patients

    ☐ Emergency patients who rebook

Financial Habits For Highly Successful Practice Owners

Having taken the reins of your new practice, you are hopefully beginning to settle into professional life as a practice owner. The practice has lived up to expectations—it's a dream come true. However, you might still have lingering doubts about whether practice revenues are going to be high enough to pay off your purchase loan, pay down the mortgage on your house, finance your children's education, give you and your family a comfortable life, and ultimately generate enough income for a phenomenal retirement.

Having worked with hundreds of people in exactly your situation, let me share some success strategies that have worked for my clients.

Live Within Your Means

Many high-income earners live paycheck to paycheck because their expenses are out of control. The more educated you become on financial matters, the more likely you will achieve financial security. Find a way to enjoy financial planning and you will have found the secret to sound money management.

Set Firm Goals

Identify and prioritize your financial goals. Do you need to renovate the clinic? Do you need to purchase or replace dental equipment? Is your home mortgage something you feel you need to pay off in the short to mid-term? Do you want to trade your car in for a new model?

Begin with the end in mind, and take some quiet time to do a visioning exercise. Put aside thoughts of money and simply imagine where you would like to be in ten, fifteen, twenty years. I call this a magic wand exercise. Wave your wand and transport yourself into the future of your dreams.

Once you have a firm idea of what you want your future life to be like, zero in on your goals, break them down into objectives, and then create a list of actions that will bring you closer to the future you desire. Now, how much do you need to earn monthly, in after-tax dollars, to finance your desired lifestyle? That figure is the target you will use when preparing your financial plan. Roadmaps are essential in business, whether a business plan, sales and marketing strategy, or a financial plan. You won't get anywhere if you don't know where you are going. A clear, firm direction with detailed objectives is not only crucial, it's motivating.

One of my clients decided he would repay his mortgage in eight years, which was an ambitious goal given the amount he owed. He wrote this goal on dozens of post-it notes and put them around his office and home. I didn't meet him until he was six years in, but he was on track to achieve his goal, and the yellow post-it notes were weathered but still visible. He told me never to underestimate the power of written goals—the fact that he saw his primary goal multiple times a day meant it was continually on his mind.

Execute Your Plan

It sounds obvious, but plans just gather dust if not immediately executed. The biggest reason for failure (planning's *Achilles' heel*) is procrastination. The way to guarantee success is to establish good financial habits from day one. Implement your goals, don't just talk about them.

Create a list of action items, such as transferring surplus funds from your practice account to your investment portfolio automatically every month. Find ways to reinforce your good habits. You have to be disciplined to embed these habits into your psyche. Ask someone, maybe your spouse, to keep you on track by monitoring your progress. Support from family is key to execution. Create systems and action plans that work for you. These could include smartphone reminders, completing weekly or monthly spreadsheets, to-do lists, automatic withdrawals, even a series of rewards—it doesn't matter as long as they work.

To begin, prepare a personal cash flow projection for the next twelve months. This spreadsheet should include anticipated income and expenses, and show disbursements such as taxes and contributions to savings.

Monitor Progress

You must find ways to track your progress regularly. For example, if you plan to transfer a percentage of your practice's surplus to your personal account to save $10,000 monthly, prepare a monthly income and expense statement that compares the target amount to the actual figure. If the amount drops below your target, you can immediately investigate the reason and take remedial action.

An excellent way to track your wealth-building efforts is to create a net worth statement regularly. Simply subtract your debts from the market value of your assets to determine your equity. It's easy, fast, and motivating.

Pay Yourself First

Paying yourself first is not ground-breaking information; financial advisors have been telling people to do this since time immemorial, but that doesn't make it any less relevant. I talked about systems earlier, and one such plan is to have your bank, or an investment advisor, automatically invest a specified amount each month from the practice account. This investment strategy is a relatively painless way to accumulate a sizable nest egg over time. To make this more palatable, start small and increase the amount gradually over time. The secret to this strategy is never to miss a payment. If the practice is short of funds one month, consider using your line of credit to make up the shortfall. The "pay yourself first" drill is a forced savings program that is hard to beat.

Invest Aggressively But Wisely

Many people invest but still lose money because their savings are tucked away "safely" in a bank term deposit earning 3%. Low returns like that will not protect you from the ravages of inflation and income tax. I urge you to find a dedicated investment advisor who can help build an equity-based stock portfolio that, over the long term, will make you in the region of 10%. I'll forgo the math, but if we assume a 3% inflation rate and a 40% tax rate, this would mean that you'd need to get a return of 5% just to remain even.

Now for the *wisely* part. Never give a broker carte blanche over your money, no matter how much you trust them, even if they are a family friend (especially if they are a family friend). Never abdicate responsibility for your investments; become educated and take a keen interest in how you invest your hard-earned money.

Now that you are a dental practice owner you will be identified as a high-income earner and therefore targeted by anyone selling financial products. Imagine sharks circling fresh meat. Have a clear financial plan and get into the habit of saying no to anything that doesn't fit your strategy perfectly. Even then, carry out exhaustive due diligence before investing a dime.

It is rarely, if ever, wise to agree to invest in non-productive activities such as loan requests from family members. Learn to politely, but firmly, say no.

Practice Sensible Buying

There is a saying that "rich people buy assets and poor people buy liabilities." I am always amazed by how many professionals I encounter who don't know the difference, or who conveniently ignore it to rationalize the desired purchase. I apologize if I am preaching to the choir, but bear with me while I clarify. An *asset* is an investment, such as real estate or equities, that generates income. Items such as boats, sports cars, and vacation properties are *liabilities* because they require cash to maintain and usually decrease in value. Assets build wealth; liabilities drain wealth.

Sensible buying doesn't necessarily mean being thrifty. You work hard and deserve an excellent lifestyle, but it makes good financial sense to delay the gratification of buying high-end luxury items until you can genuinely afford them.

Reward Yourself!

Running a clinic, while at the same time seeing patients all day, can at first seem like a dream come true, but it can soon turn into a daily grind if that's all there is to your life. If you are going to sustain your enthusiasm and energy, your life can't feel like drudgery. You have to know that you are working for something more imminent than a wealthy early retirement. Rewarding yourself works well. As part of your financial plan, identify the "prizes" you would like to receive for reaching preset goals. If your dream is to own a Porsche or stay at a Four Seasons in Mexico or Hawaii for a couple of weeks every year, build that into your plan. As long as the rewards are commensurate with the practice's financial gains and ability to pay you, go for it. Don't worry about money all the time; have some fun.

You deserve it!

Key Takeaways

- [ ] From the day you take over the clinic every action you take will make the practice more or less profitable. Start as you mean to go on—in control.

- [ ] Focus on growth from day one. Meet with the office manager, or equivalent, within the first week.

- [ ] Live within your means. Become financially savvy.

- [ ] Set firm goals. Identify and prioritize your financial goals.

☐ Execute your plan. The most significant cause of failure is procrastination.

☐ Monitor progress. Never take your eye off the ball. Review the clinic's financial statements every month.

☐ Pay yourself first. Have an investment strategy.

☐ Invest aggressively but wisely. Investments that don't provide enough return to break-even don't make sense.

☐ Buy sensibly and delay gratification until you can afford what you want. Assets build wealth; liabilities drain wealth.

☐ Reward yourself. Understand that you are working for something more imminent than a wealthy early retirement.

Acknowledgements

First, I'd like to thank Mike Wicks, my collaborator on this book. He helped me find my voice and made the book both readable and accessible. His commitment and passion for the book were motivating. He helped make the whole process enjoyable and a lot easier than I ever thought possible.

Thank you to the Blue Beetle Books publishing team. Paul Abra for handling production and promotion, Tom Spetter for designing such an amazing jacket and for laying the book out with such style, Kara Anderson for her considerable copyediting skills, Sheila Wicks for proofreading the final manuscript to ensure there were no embarrassing typos, and finally Mike Wicks for his ongoing publishing guidance.

Finally, I want to thank my wife Marie for her encouragement and unconditional support. Without her, I would never have been able to write this book.

Notes:

Notes:

Notes:

Notes:

Notes:

www.ingramcontent.com/pod-product-compliance
Lightning Source LLC
Chambersburg PA
CBHW071717210326
41597CB00017B/2510

9 781777 828721